MR. ED: DEAD

AND OTHER
OBITUARIES

OF THE
**MOST
FAMOUS
PEOPLE**

WHO
**NEVER
LIVED**

BARRY NELSON *AND* **TOM SCHECKER**

sourcebooks

Published by Sourcebooks, Inc.
P.O. Box 4410, Naperville, Illinois 60567-4410
(630) 961-3900
Fax: (630) 961-2168
www.sourcebooks.com

Library of Congress Cataloging-in-Publication Data
Nelson, Barry.
  Mr. Ed: dead : and other obituaries of the most famous people who never lived / Barry Nelson, Tom Schecker.
     p. cm.
  1. Obituaries--Humor. 2. Popular culture--Humor. I. Schecker, Tom. II. Title.
  PN6231.O25N45 2010
  818'.602--dc22
                                    2009051841

Printed and bound in the United States of America
       VP 10 9 8 7 6 5 4 3 2 1

BARRY:

For my beautiful wife and best friend Amy, who
shares my sense of humor and is the best thing
that ever happened to me. For my sons Colin and
Simon, of whom I am endlessly proud and impressed.
For my parents Jim and Gelsi Nelson, and in-laws
Skip and Helen Chandler-Dad and Helen, I miss you
and wish you could be here to see this.

TOM:

For my Mom, Dad, and Karen.

Acknowledgments

The authors would like to thank Nicole Diamond Austin for being an early proponent of the book; the irrepressible wordsmith, advocate, and publicist extraordinaire Jim Eber; our agent David Fugate of Launchbooks, who immediately recognized the potential of *Mr. Ed: Dead* and brought it to Sourcebooks. Thanks to the Sourcebooks team: editor Peter Lynch, publicist Carrie Gellin, and Ashley Haag and Anne Hartman for understanding and executing our vision. Special thanks to those who copyedited the book and let us leave in the word "Etymologists" because we thought it was funnier than "Entomologists."

Thanks to Nan Satter, whose generous review and comments nudged us onto the right path; Ellen Roberts of Where Books Begin whose early advice prepared us for the road ahead; and Natasha Francis, for helping us assemble the material and shepherd wayward characters back into the manuscript. Thanks to Matt and Siris for Sip in NYC, a good place to work on a book.

We'd like to thank the team of *Mr. Ed: Dead* guinea pigs for their feedback on early portions of the manuscript: Barbara Appleby, John Arbucci, Charlyne Biggs, Becky Edwards, Robin Meyer Fremont, David Gibson, Amanda Goodwin, Rosy Macedo, Amy Morrison, Donna Ng, John and Cindy Nelson, Laura Schecker, Mom and Dad Schecker, Sharon Schecker, and Daren Winckel.

Thanks go to our college compatriots Paul Ferris, Rick Fremont, and David Krietzberg, three of the funniest people we've ever had the honor to know.

An extra-special thank you to our families for their undying patience and support while we spent countless hours on Skype laughing, writing, and often working. Guidance from Amy and Karen saved us from literary ruin a bunch of times. We do love them madly.

MR. ED: DEAD

HOLLYWOOD, Calif. — Palomino gelding TV star and talking horse, Mr. Ed, has died. He was 34. Ed, born Bamboo Harvester in Greensboro, KY, was the longtime companion of architect Wilbur Post. Post designed and built a special stable in his home, where Mr. Ed stayed for much of the 1960s.

Ed's television career ended in 1966. A modeling career followed, primarily as a unicorn in posters marketed to preteen girls. In 1967, he appeared in the classic spaghetti Western *I Crudeli (The Hellbenders)*. Known for his wry sense of humor, Mr. Ed inked a deal to appear with Charles Bronson in *Chino*.

During a delay in shooting of the Western, the talking horse accepted an offer he couldn't refuse from Francis Ford Coppola to do a cameo role in *The Godfather*. Mr. Ed did not read the fine print in the contract, which specified that only his head would appear in the film, or else he likely would not have agreed to the scene that lead to his death. Sadly, a chemical error in the film-processing lab destroyed Mr. Ed's scenes. Coppola reshot the scenes with 1950s movie idol Black Beauty.

TRAGIC MURDER-SUICIDE AT GOLDEN GATE BRIDGE

Dick, Jane & Spot Dead

SAN FRANCISCO *(San Francisco Chronicle)* —
Dick said, "Jump, Jane, jump!"
Jane jumped.
Dick said, "Jump, Spot!"
Spot said, "Bark! Bark!"
Spot jumped.
Dick was sad.
"Oh, oh, oh. What have I done?"
Dick jumped, too.
The policeman said: "This is not fun. No, no, no.
Mother, Father, Tim, and Puff will be sad."

JOE CAMEL, 92
TOBACCO FIRM MOURNS LOSS OF DROMEDARY-ABOUT-TOWN

RALEIGH, N.C. (AP) — Joe Camel died at Philip Morris Medical Center yesterday. "We're flummoxed—Joe was in terrific shape. I just saw him at the RJR Smoking Lounge yesterday," said a R. J. Reynolds spokesman.

Rumors that the icon had been suffering from emphysema, pulmonary edema, heart disease, and cancerous lesions on the hump for 10 years were, according to the spokesman, "A pack of lies—he was a robust 92 and probably had another 20 years in him."

Camel retired from his position representing the merits of youthful tobacco addiction in 1997 and went into hiding after consumer groups threatened his life. He surfaced in Asia, performing philanthropic pursuits consisting chiefly of handing out free bundles of cigarettes to children in Vietnam, Laos, and Thailand.

Camel will be cremated after being treated with a thousand toxic chemicals and rolled in thin, fast-combusting paper.

PILLSBURY DOUGHBOY CRITICAL

Half-Baked Prank Leaves 'Poppin' Fresh,' the Pillsbury Doughboy, in Critical Condition, Doctors Say

MINNEAPOLIS (AP) — A twisted prank by the Hamburger Helper Helping Hand and Speedy the Alka Seltzer Boy has put Poppin' Fresh in the burn unit of the Maypo Clinic. Speedy confessed that he lured the doughboy into the Pillsbury Corporate office "jacuzzi," promising, "Oh, what a relief it is." Accomplice Helping Hand then pushed the doughboy into a vat of boiling Crisco.

Fresh is listed in tender, flaky condition at St. Elmo's.

"He has a delectable golden crust over 80 percent of his body," Dr. Renato Focaccia told reporters at a press conference. Speedy and Helping Hand are being held pending a hearing before Judge Sara Lee.

BETTY CROCKER DEAD AT 88; RICH BUT NO LONGER MOIST

Was Successful Marketer Despite Inability to Think Outside of the Box

MINNEAPOLIS (AP) — Kitchen icon Betty Crocker failed to rise this morning. She was 88. She was the go-to gal for one-box sensations that sated hungry husbands everywhere. Crocker was a good cook too. In her will, she asked to be mixed with 2 eggs and $1/2$ cup oil, mixed for 3 minutes on high speed, spread evenly, topped with walnuts, and cremated at 1350 degrees for 45 minutes.

Enraged Dentist Hunts Down Count Chocula, Age 355

Drives Wooden Spoon Through Heart

POPPIN' FRESH IS TOAST

QUICK RISE TO SUCCESS MARKED LIFE OF PILLSBURY DOUGHBOY, DEAD AT 43

MINNEAPOLIS (UPI) — Fragrant American icon Poppin' Fresh is being remembered as a jolly, helpful friend in the kitchen. Fresh had been recuperating from burns at the Maypo Clinic as a result of a prank gone wrong. Fresh was pronounced dead when a poke to the stomach failed to elicit his signature giggle. The Pillsbury Doughboy will be torn to pieces and fed to the ducks.

You Can't Get Anything You Want

GREAT BARRINGTON, Mass. — Alice, counter cultural icon and local restaurateur, died on Thanksgiving Day at Herbal Karma Health Care Center. Alice had been rushed to the Center earlier this week, by horse cart, once the phase of the moon made a trip to the health center auspicious.

Former customers of the restaurant said they were not surprised. Alice had been losing weight for years and had lately done so at an alarming rate. Ethical and health concerns drove her to increasingly restrictive diets.

The restaurant, popular since the early 1960s, saw its menu grow sparse over the years.

Longtime employee Dishwasher Dave adjusted his bandanna and nursed a marijuana cigarette as he chronicled Alice's descent into decency:

1973: Alice stops eating red meat. Drops burgers from menu. Poultry followed shortly thereafter. All things with feet and face are now suspect.

1974: Bacon linked to cancer. Alice amends breakfast menu.

1977: Alice becomes a pescetarian and revels in her new fish offerings.

1981: Mercury concentrations cause Alice to strike fish from menu. Converts to lacto-ovo vegetarianism. Customers begin to worry.

1983: Took advantage of quiche craze and made fortune.

1991: Alice removes eggs from menu to protest slaughter of unwanted male chicks. Stops milk orders after discovering that cows find cold milking equipment on udders uncomfortable. Gives 10 percent of profits to PETA.

1995: Switches to all-blender cuisine and serves everything in cups to avoid wasting water on dishwashing. Dishwasher Dave protests and Blue Plate Specials return.

1996: Blue Plate Specials changed to Green Plate Specials as Alice's Restaurant changes name to Alice's Vegetarian Restaurant.

2000: Now a strict vegan, Alice removes all food from menu that tastes good. Business takes turn for the worse.

2003: Alice meets Michio Kushi and converts to macrobiotic cooking. Menu offerings: seaweed and brown rice.

Friends say that Alice, a plump flower child in the mid-1960s, was now down to a heroin-chic 105 pounds. After a visit to a New Mexico spa for a cleansing, Alice was an emaciated waif. In 2004 she read an article in *High Times* magazine, which revealed that plants have a physiological response to music. Alice developed a profound awareness for the feelings and emotions of plant life and vowed to become a fruitarian.

The next day, all vegetable matter was removed from the menu. Then, in solidarity with migrant pickers, Alice also took fruit off the menu. Business suffered, and Alice became chronically weak.

By Tuesday, regular customers were offered the only thing left on Alice's menu: hot water. She lost consciousness on Thanksgiving Day and never recovered.

Following her wishes, there will be a short service in the middle of the Bethel Woods, after which Alice will be composted.

BOBBY McGEE, 56

Had Nothin' Left to Lose,
But Still Managed to Lose His Life

VENICE BEACH, Calif. (UPI) — Blues singer Bobby McGee has been found dead in his home—a Volkswagen Microbus. According to friends, he had been feeling good, which was good enough for Bobby McGee. He did not look good, however, when found on a cot behind the wall of beads in his van.

McGee became a fixture on the Venice Beach boardwalk in 1972, after hitchhik-

ing from New Orleans. Somewhere near Salinas, Calif., he told the truck driver and his travel companion that he was tired of rambling and was looking for a home. He found it in a parking lot at Venice Beach.

The singer, a diabetic, was instructed by his doctor to avoid eating greasy boardwalk food. Official cause of death is a six-pack of beer and a bucket of chicken.

Friends clearing out the microbus found lyrics to a song Bobby was working on. It said he was "ready to trade in all my yesterdays for a single tomorrow..."

And that's exactly what he did, with an extra crispy chicken leg in one hand and Lowenbrau in the other.

HOT TUB SHOCKER

Bionic Man and Woman Electrocuted while on Romantic Vacation

Pentagon Official: "We can't rebuild them!"

STROUDSBURG, Pa. — Steve Austin, 44, and Jaime Sommers-Austin, 43, were found dead in their suite at Caligula Honeymoon Resort. The couple had been celebrating their five-year wedding anniversary. From all accounts, they had been at the top of their game: better, stronger, and faster.

The smell of burning rubber and tread marks on local mountain roads indicate the couple had gone for a run prior to their bath. But it was the enjoyment of connubial pleasures that proved fatal to the multi-million-dollar couple as they enjoyed a soak in their suite's hot tub.

Investigators believe the application of a graphite-based personal lubricant and faulty gonadal grafting produced an effect similar to a radio being dropped into a bathtub. System failure was catastrophic, which leads investigators to conclude that the Johnson Controls pleasure sensor installed in Mr. Austin had been set beyond recommended limits, perhaps by Mrs. Austin. The incident dispels rumors that Jamie Sommers-Austin, cryogenically frozen and revived in 1977, was permanently frigid.

The Six Million Dollar Man and his Six Million Dollar Wife had a twelve-million-dollar insurance deductible. A hospital spokesman said, "The adjuster totaled them, so they will be sold for parts."

A Bottle of Red, A Bottle of White & A Sad Tragedy on Long Island

SYOSSET, N.Y. (UPI) — Brenda Malgieri and Eddie Civetti, both 47, were thrown from Eddie's Mustang convertible after he swerved off the road last night.

Brenda and Eddie, who were popular steadies in high school, had a tumultuous and short-lived marriage in 1975. A waiter at their favorite Italian restaurant reported that prior to the accident, the duo sat for hours at a table near the street consuming a bottle of red and a bottle of white.

An EMT on the scene exclaimed, "The best we could do was pick up their pieces!"

Brenda, an aerobics instructor to the stars, had recently said goodbye to Hollywood and moved out to Long Island with her husband Anthony, who works in a grocery store. Eddie was a big shot in real estate who had been married to an uptown girl for the longest time, until she filed for divorce and moved to Allentown.

Friends and family always thought Brenda and Eddie would both find a way to survive—without each other. But Eddie did not enjoy the role of the stranger, so he moved half a mile away from Brenda. Husband Anthony, a rather innocent man, was philosophical about his loss. "I'm only human, so I'm keepin' the faith. For Brenda and me, it's always been a matter of trust, and this is the time for forgiveness. She'll always be a woman to me, 'cause honesty is what I value in my life. You may be right, I may be crazy, but I loved her just the way she was."

The piano man at Captain Jack's Bar in Oyster Bay, Bill Martin, was one of the first to arrive on the scene. The entertainer said: "I remember those days hanging out on the village green with those two. Don't ask me why, but only the good die young." Friends are asked to gather for a double funeral at St. Virginia's Church Saturday at 3:05 to wave Brenda and Eddie goodbye.

Industrial Accident Silences Perky Cereal Elves

GIANT MILK SPILL AT WISCONSIN FACTORY SATURATES SNAP, CRACKLE & POP

Public Invited to All-You-Can Eat Memorial Service

TWO RIVERS, Wisc. (AP) — On tour promoting their latest memoir, *Sweet Noise of Success*, Snap, Crackle & Pop were caught in a deluge of whole milk and succumbed to sogginess. They were flown to a toasting facility in Battle Creek, Mich., but could not be reconstituted.

The accident happened when Pop, the playful younger brother of the elfin trio, mischievously opened a valve on a 100,000-gallon tank destined for a fried cheddar curd factory. Several workers and company executives were also drenched in milk, but because of human cell structure, the liquid merely beaded up on their skin and dripped off.

Kraft Foods has kindly donated 300 pounds of marshmallows for entombment of the beloved rice-based gnomes. The public is invited to a memorial service for Snap, Crackle & Pop on Sunday morning. Light and chewy refreshments will be served.

Fat Albert, All-Time Buck Buck World Champion, Has Died

PHILADELPHIA — Fat Albert died in Philadelphia last Tuesday. Throughout his life, Mr. Albert had been warned that his tremendous weight would shorten his life. He was 97.

Although never dipping below the quarter-ton mark, Mr. Albert outlived three primary care physicians, two nutritionists, and four physical therapists. His heart, which had grown to the size of a basketball, will go on display at the Buck Buck Hall of Fame in Philadelphia. Experts in sports medicine who studied the organ have revised nutrition guidelines for players, which include a marked increase in lard and hydrogenated fats.

Fat Albert Medical History

As part of the study on the importance of Fat Albert's techniques for prolonging life and increasing athletic ability, his family sanctioned the release of his medical records:

1979: Diagnosed with high blood pressure

1980: Dangerously high cholesterol

1987: Severe case of diabetes

1999: Varicose veins and poor circulation

2000: Banned for life from Old Country Buffet

2006: Chafing

2015: Enlarged heart

2017: Enlarged liver

2019: Enlarged everything else

2031: Massive liposuction; loses 455 pounds

2032: Able to change own socks

2033: Gains 480 pounds after receiving Cinnabon credit card

2041: Finds remote control from 1985 Zenith color TV in folds of belly

2045: Acid reflux melts tracksuit

2053: Bed sores the size of dinner plates, and vice versa

2058: Has jaw wired with rebar as part of weight-loss regime

2060: Ate sundae to celebrate loss of 500th pound

2061: *Biggest Loser* Lifetime Achievement Award: Season 57

RALPH KRAMDEN, 49

BUS DRIVER TURNED INVENTOR DIES AFTER RECEIVING FIRST ROYALTY CHECK

QUEENS, N.Y. (UPI) — Former Brooklyn bus driver Ralph Kramden, 49, died yesterday of a heart attack. He passed away minutes after receiving his first royalty check for his invention, the "Kramden Kruise Kontrol." The device allowed him to drive his bus by using only the brake pedal. Ford Motor Company paid the hefty Kramden a hefty sum for the device. Suddenly, bang, zoom, his fortunes went right to the moon. Alice Kramden said that upon opening the envelope containing the check (reportedly for $100,000), Kramden murmured "Hommena hommena hommena hommena" and then keeled over dead.

LUCILLE ESMERALDA McGILLICUDDY RICARDO

WIFE OF BAND LEADER DIES IN BULLET FACTORY

NEW YORK (UPI) — Lucy Ricardo, wife of famous band leader Ricky Ricardo, died in an explosion at the Brooklyn Navy Yard Bullet Factory late last night. Mrs. Ricardo's neighbor Ethel Mertz was also killed.

Mr. Ricardo and Mr. Mertz had no explanation for what their wives were doing at the bullet factory. Factory manager Harrison Marx explained that the two women had just joined the company and were spending their first day on the bullet assembly line.

"They said they had assembly line experience at a chocolate factory.", said Mr. Marx. "But apparently they couldn't keep up. We found bullets in their pockets, in their aprons, in their hair. But why the hell would you put bullets in your mouth?"

Security photo taken minutes before the accident

Local Man Trips over Ottoman, Breaks Neck

Rob Petrie Dead at 47

NEWS PRODUCER KILLED BY ENRAGED BOSS

Mary Richards Bludgeoned with Daytime Emmy Trophy by Exasperated News Director

She's Not Going to Make It After All

Flying Nun Violates D.C. Airspace, Shot Down

Capital Evacuated; Mother Superior Cross

WASHINGTON, D.C. — The Flying Nun triggered a red alert at the White House yesterday, along with the frantic evacuation of the Capitol and the Supreme Court, before being shot down by an Air Force F-16. Sister Bertrille had been flying from Puerto Rico to New York to visit a sick child when she drifted into D.C. air space. According to the FAA, she had not filed a flight plan.

A Pentagon official said the defense secretary, a Methodist, was contacted and gave the shoot-down order. The now-declassified mission code name was "What's Black and White and Red All Over?"

Pilot of the F-16, Captain Pete Mitchell, described the incident: "We were scrambled at 14:37 Eastern time and picked the bogey up about 12 miles southeast of Washington. The pilot refused to respond to numerous radio calls, and we were forced to engage. My wingman and I initially thought this would be pretty easy, shooting down a nun wearing only a habit and large hat. But she was tough. Due to her extremely slow speed, we flew right past her on our first pass. And our missiles proved useless. A flying nun produces no heat signature for the Sidewinders, and at 90 pounds, there's no radar lock. On our final pass, we switched to guns. The 50-millimeter Gatling proved very effective on the intruding Sister. I just thank God we had them."

In San Juan, the mother superior for the San Taco Convent said that the Order was deeply saddened but not surprised. "The girl never listened; she never followed orders. Maybe this will teach her a lesson."

Space Shuttle Windshield Damaged by Giant Moth While Flying Over Japan

Burning Wings and Guts Shower City Below; Incident Angers Giant Fire-Breathing Lizard

Local Man Dies on First Screen

Police report that a local man was killed yesterday while eating dots. The unsuspecting victim had just picked up some fruit when a red ghost approached and killed him with a single touch. He is survived by his wife, Mrs. PacMan.

RECENT DEATHS

Fester—Adverse chemical reaction to new energy-efficient light bulbs. Uncle to Morticia Addams. Has been dead many times before. Feeling better now.

Grandpa Munster—Genuine heart attack this time. Survived by two boxes of handmade Macanudo cigars.

Hi Friends and Family of the Bradys!

As I write this letter, it is probably freezing where you are, but Sam the Butcher and I are sipping Bahama Mamas in a tropical paradise! Things have gotten a little complicated.

I guess my frustration has been welling up for years, but this Thanksgiving, it finally came to a head.

After those six little brats left, it was only Mike, Carol, and me in the house, which was fine. But then there were the reunions. And the family trips. The spouses, girlfriends, boyfriends, and all that laundry. Every holiday, these people still brought their laundry back for me to do! Do you think at least one of them could learn to separate the whites?

That's not the only dirty laundry. Come on! How could they all pretend not to notice what was up with Mike. Always with the trips to Hawaii, getting "accidentally" separated from Carol for hours at a time aboard the Love Boat—and all those camping trips! Hellooo! Gaaaayy! Of course, Carol isn't going to say anything; it just makes it easier for her to be with Greg! And Marcia, Marcia, Marcia! More rolled-up $100 bills came out of her jeans than in a Studio 54 bathroom! Peter, he had aspirations to be as cool as Humphrey Bogart and the smarmy little s**t works in an office! I'm sorry, that was uncalled for.

I will miss Bobby. Sweet little Bobby.

As I slaved over turkey dinner for 20 (without any help), Bobby told me his secret plan to drop out of college to take up stock car racing. Cindy was whining about not being able to go on another ski trip with her friends where she wanted to try out her new IUD. Jan is probably the most stable of the Brady bunch, and I think she could have gone on to do great things. But she's the one who dropped the gravy boat. I guess I sort of snapped.

From what I remember, I was standing at the end of the table, carving knife in hand, ready to slice the turkey. They were all talking at once, as usual, when crash! A quart of my best turkey gravy, not a single lump, all over the rug. I took Jan's head off with one swift motion. The rest felt like I was watching Enter the Dragon, only I was Bruce Lee.

After I came to, I called Sam, and he helped me clean everything up. A girl can learn something about blood stains from a butcher! I rifled through Mike's sock drawer and found the key to his secret little beach house here on the island. Oh, don't even try to find us. We've changed our appearance, and we don't go out in public. Our housekeeper does all the shopping.

Sam did a great job of wrapping all the parts in butcher paper.

Happy Holidays!

Aloha!
Alice Nelson

HAZEL

MAID

1918–1967

DID I LEAVE
THE IRON ON?

LOCAL MARINE MAKES THE GRADE

MOUNT PILOT, N.C. (*The Pilot*) — The people of Mayberry are beaming with pride to learn that their own Gomer Pyle has received a prestigious promotion from the U.S. Marine Corps. Private Pyle has joined the Marine's elite bomb-disposal unit. This newspaper predicts that Gomer's career is about to explode!

Private Pyle

7 p.m. **Saturday**

3 My Two Sons
Starring Fred MacMurray
Tune in next week when Dad and the boys bury Chip! Steve, Robbie, and Ernie try to get ready for Chip's funeral, but Uncle Charlie burns the pancakes!

Sherlock Holmes, 68, Private Investigator

Cause of Death a Mystery

LONDON — Sherlock Holmes, 68, of Baker Street, was found dead in the street in front of his home in the early morning hours. Inspector LeStrade of Scotland Yard gathered information and has formulated a hypothesis on the cause of death.

LeStrade records the facts as follows: A coach containing a woman in a black lace veil was seen in the vicinity of Baker Street the prior evening. Hairs retrieved from Holmes's trousers match those of Mrs. Hudson's cat, a Persian longhair. The deceased was clutching a newspaper with the headline "Scandal in Bohemia." There was exactly one pound, fifty pence in his front right pocket. In the left pocket of his woolen overcoat, a still-smoldering pipe filled with Latakia tobacco from Cyprus. In the next street, a black hound has been howling for several days. It was not foggy on the morning of the incident, but it had rained overnight. A man in an apron was seen in front of the butcher's sweeping the sidewalk but disappeared when police arrived.

LeStrade has concluded from the evidence that Holmes was initially poisoned with strychnine in a pub, possibly by his landlady. When he failed to die, the amateur detective was chased through the dark streets of London for several hours and shot with a pistol. The inspector postulates that Holmes' corpse was moved from the location of death and placed at the foot of 221-B in the early hours of the morning. The killer then lit Holmes' pipe, placed a newspaper in the dead man's hand, and sped off in a hansom cab. LeStrade has put London officers on alert and vows to catch the killer, whom he suspects is the Czech ambassador acting on behalf of the Hungarian secret police.

(continued on next page)

(continued from previous page)

Dr. John Watson disputed the inspector's findings. "The only mystery here is how LeStrade retains his job. He is a bloody imbecile. Holmes and I were across the street at the newsstand. He bought a paper. As we crossed the road, a cat ran in his path and he tripped into the street. The old boy was run over by a carriage. Good heavens, at least 50 people witnessed the accident! The wheel marks across his back are as plain as day."

EMPEROR DIES OF HYPOTHERMIA IN SPITE OF NEW CLOTHES

PAGE 3 GIRLS:
"WE CAN RELATE!"

Professor Plum Murdered by Colonel Mustard in Dining Room With Candlestick

LONDON (Reuters) — Scotland Yard reports that Cambridge professor Peter Plum was murdered Friday night in the dining room at Boddy Mansion in the Midlands. Col. Algernon Mustard is charged with the slaying. His fingerprints were found on a candlestick, which had been missing from the hall. A lead pipe was found clenched in Plum's hand. The salon window was open, and there were dirty footprints on the carpet. Cat footprints.

Witnesses Miss Vivienne Scarlet and Mrs. Henrietta Peacock discovered Plum's body, allegedly after spending the afternoon in the billiard room. Curiously, Ms. Scarlett arrived for dinner carrying a length of rope and Mrs. Peacock a revolver. They asserted that a pheasant had escaped from the kitchen and that they were merely trying to capture it.

The housekeeper, Mrs. White, was in the conservatory at the time, wielding a wrench, which she claimed to have used to fix a broken faucet. Sgt. Grey of Scotland Yard notes that the conservatory doesn't have a faucet, and anyway, most of the plants are dead.

Murder most foul has been a recurring theme at the Boddy Mansion as of late. Last Tuesday, Rev. Randolph Green was found stabbed in the ballroom with a dagger. Monsieur Alphonse Brunette was charged with the slaying, although he is armless.

Heir to the Boddy fortune, the notorious Dr. Black, was recently murdered in the library with poison. Since then, dinner guests have avoided the red wine, hand-picked from the cellar by the deceased, a noted chemist.

Police report that the only person who is not a suspect and has been completely forthcoming about the slayings is the butler.

Town Sued Over Shooting

MAYBERRY R.F.D. — The town of Mayberry has been named in a complaint filed by the estate of Beatrice Taylor for wrongful death, according to County Clerk Howard Sprague. Also named in the suit is Sheriff Andy Taylor.

The suit stems from the tragic and accidental shooting of Miss Taylor, known as Aunt Bea, by then Deputy Sheriff Fife. Fife had been showing his gun to Opie Taylor, son of Sheriff Taylor, in the Taylor's kitchen when it discharged. Aunt Bea, who was cooking a batch of her famous fried chicken at the time, was struck once in the neck and pronounced dead by Doc Wallace at the scene. The chicken was never finished, much to the chagrin of Sheriff Taylor.

In the suit, the estate of Miss Taylor claims that the town and the sheriff behaved in a "grossly negligent" manner by allowing Mr. Fife to carry a firearm. The suit claims that "Deputy Sheriff Fife was a well-known bumbler and widely recognized buffoon. He had a long history of inadvertently discharging his weapon." It continues, "No one in their right mind would have let this person carry a gun."

The suit points out that the only firearms training Fife had ever received was from Mayberry's own Gomer Pyle.

Mr. Fife remains in custody, having inadvertently locked himself in the town jail.

Deputy Sheriff Fife

Unidentified Man Found in Incinerated Aston Martin

FIRE BRIGADE HELD AT BAY FOR NEARLY AN HOUR BY EXPLODING BULLETS, ROCKETS, AND MONT BLANC PENS

MAYFAIR, England — After removing the remains of an unidentified man, Mayfair police were shocked to discover the lethal customizations that had been made to the sports car.

The Aston Martin DB9 had been extensively modified with bullet-proof glass, bumper-mounted machine guns, rocket launchers, wheel blades, a smoke-generating machine, and an oil-slick sprayer. The car also contained a martini shaker.

Investigators report that the fire started when the car's ejection seat was activated, but its retractable roof was not.

Several yards away, investigators recovered the victim's right arm still handcuffed to a briefcase. Attempts to open the high-tech attaché have been unsuccessful but did start a digital timer on the outside of the case. Police believe the case will unlock itself in 36 hours when the timer goes off.

DATE: APRIL 6, 1979, BY 86021-FWB

IMPOSSIBLE MISSIONS FORCE CONFIDENTIAL REPORT
SUBJECT: Death of James Phelps, 50, Government Agent
1. According to Agent ▓▓▓▓▓▓▓ from FBI Los Angeles
office, March 21 was not a good morning for Mr. Phelps.
Upon the receipt of orders from a recovered IMF tape
recorder at approximately 7 a.m. at MacArthur Park on
Bench #4756 next to granite rock #887, Phelps decided
not to accept that week's impossible mission. His
decision initiated termination instructions in the
Wollensak 380Z mini tape machine.

2. Five seconds later, according to IMF protocol,
not only did the tape machine self-destruct but the
bench did too. Any shred of evidence concerning
the ▓▓▓▓▓▓▓ affair and the investigation into the
Church of ▓▓▓▓▓▓▓▓ and connections to members of
Hollywood's communist party circle no longer exists.
Division Seven Chief ▓▓▓▓▓▓▓ has already notified
the director of Phelps' "decision" in order for him to
publicly deny any knowledge of the incident. The FBI
has assured us that Secretary ▓▓▓▓▓▓▓▓ is generally
oblivious anyway, so he could pass a lie detector test
if necessary. The dossier on the Hollywood chapter of
the Church of ▓▓▓▓▓▓▓ has been destroyed and all of
its photos returned to *The Enquirer* newspaper.

3. A reliable source told Agent ▓▓▓▓▓▓▓ that he
recovered a rubber mask with likeness of author ▓▓▓▓▓▓,
a hairpiece, a high-caliber weapon, a copy of
Dianetics, an ascot, and part of a white short-sleeved
shirt. IMF makeup artist Rollin Hand did, indeed,
confirm that Mr. Phelps was in possession of the rubber
disguise of the author, an FBI informant. Agent Cinnamon
Carter (retired) confirmed the identity of Phelps's
underwear fragments. Agent ▓▓▓▓▓▓▓ has entrusted
the LA County Coroner's Office with physical evidence,
acknowledging that the LACCO's incompetence in handling
such evidence will ensure that the public will never
know the identity or mission of the deceased.

Lancelot Link, Formerly Secret Chimp, Poisoned at Restaurant

LONDON (*The London Times*) — Scotland Yard has accused Russia of poisoning London resident Lancelot Link at a popular restaurant in Dover. Large amounts of polonium-210 were found in the banana split consumed by Link during a casual lunch meeting with a Russian bear. Link was 24.

Police identified the assassin as an undercover member of the KRASS (Kovert Russian Animal Secret Snoopers). The secretive agency is notorious in spy circles for its use of the Polonium Ice Cream Sundae.

Link was recently "outed" as an American spy by a newspaper columnist. This followed the publication of an op-ed written by Link's wife, Mata Hairi. Her piece in the *Times* was critical of the administration's use of the term *macaca* to refer to operatives from APE (Agency to Prevent Evil).

The Chimp-in-Chief promised to act decisively regarding such leaks by pardoning anyone who knowingly reveals the identity of a covert agent. The poisoning of Link has caused a cooling in relations between the two countries, which are currently having a summit in the president's ancestral land, the Democratic Republic of Congo. He issued a statement expressing sorrow over the loss of Agent Link and promised that he would look into the soul of his counterpart to see if he got it wrong and maybe the Russian can't be trusted. He plans to meet the Russian premier over dessert.

Space Agency Loses Contact With Mars-Bound Rocket Piloted by Intellectually Gifted Pooch and Bird-Brained Companion

NOORDWIJK, Netherlands (AP) — "Rats, I think we've lost him," a spokesperson for ESTEC declared yesterday. Col. Snoopy and Maj. Woodstock had lifted off from the European Space Agency after weeks in astronaut obedience school. The crew has extensive experience with space flight, having flown a mission in 1969 aboard the Apollo 10 lunar module. Snoopy, a WWI flying ace, wrote extensively of his dogfights against the Red Baron in a memoir titled *Sniffing Behind Enemy Lines*.

The space agency attempted to communicate with the Mars probe for two and a half days and today alerted the public that they hadn't heard a peep from the navigator, Maj. Woodstock. Engineers fear that the Royal typewriter Col. Snoopy insisted on bringing may have dislodged, incapacitating the crew.

Bereavement T-shirts have already been spotted that read "Sadness is a Cold Puppy."

GOOD GRIEF! PSYCHIATRIST LUCY VAN PELT FOUND DEAD IN OFFICE

ST. PAUL, Minn. (UPI) — St. Paul's most inexpensive psychiatrist, Lucy van Pelt, was found dead in her office yesterday. The 65-year-old doctor was renowned for charging only 5 cents per session.

Police say Dr. van Pelt appears to have been pummeled with an old deflated football, which had been left lodged in her throat. According to the coroner's report, a kicking tee was recovered from another part of the victim's anatomy.

Lassie, Episode 412: Bad Dog!

FADE IN: A KITCHEN IN THE MIDWEST.
Timmy's mom is preparing dinner.
Lassie unlocks door with
key clenched in teeth.

TIMMY'S MOM:
Lassie! Timmy hasn't come home tonight.
Didn't you and Timmy go off chasing a fox?

LASSIE:
Ruff!

TIMMY'S MOM:
Did you chase it over the ridge
to the old Wellesley place?

LASSIE:
Ruff!

TIMMY'S MOM:
But that barn is about to fall down.
Did the fox go in the barn?

LASSIE:
Ruff!

TIMMY'S MOM:
Oh no! That rickety old thing
could come down at any minute.
Did Timmy go in the barn?

LASSIE:
Ruff!

TIMMY'S MOM:
Was the barn OK?

LASSIE:
[Whine]

TIMMY'S MOM:
Oh no. Lassie!
Did the barn fall down?

LASSIE:
Ruff!

TIMMY'S MOM:
Did the barn fall down on...Timmy?

LASSIE:
Ruff!

TIMMY'S MOM:
Oh, Lassie. That was hours ago!
You didn't go on chasing the fox
and leave Timmy to die, did you?

Lassie:
[Crawls under bed.]
FADE OUT

BBC Loses Dog

WENSLEYDALE — We regret to announce that Gromit, the popular co-star of the Wallace & Gromit series, is dead. Gromit's veterinary doctor reports the cause of death as an intestinal blockage that occurred after his patient mistook a lump of clay for a piece of cheese.

BENJI, DEAD AT 8 (56)

ORLANDO, Fla. (UPI) — Tragedy struck the Disney Studios today when the popular and adorable canine star Benji was run over by Herbie the Love Bug. Studio police ruled the incident an accident and Herbie was not charged. However, overwhelmed by grief, he had to be towed home.

WILBUR, 22
SOME DEAD PIG

(AP) — Wilbur, porcine confidant of Charlotte the Spider, died in his sleep last night. Farmer Zuckerman reported that Wilbur was 22 years old. An intelligent blue-ribbon winner at 4-H events, the razorback was, however, considered by many members of the swine community to be a boar.

Eerily, the farmer's daughter, who discovered the body, was alerted to Wilbur's demise by a spider web woven above his pen that read "Some Dead Pig." The Zuckermans have promised to give Wilbur a proper send-off.

Rotary Club Meat Raffle

244 pounds, various cuts of pork for freezer.

Tickets $5, available at Zuckerman's Farm.

Herbie the Love Bug Dead at 40

Mechanic: Autotopsy Rules Out Foul Play in Steering Wheel

ORLANDO, Fla. (UPI) — Disney Studios report that Herbie the Love Bug died today in an apparent suicide. He was 40. Friends of the sexy, popular VW say that Herbie had been suffering from severe depression since accidentally running over Benji two weeks ago. Herbie was found alone in his garage with the door closed and his engine running.

In Memoriam

Green eggs and ham
Killed Sam-I-am
I warned him, damn, I did so ma'am!

I warned poor Sam that danger lies
In foods whose hue surely belies
The nature of their normal state
Sitting on the breakfast plate.

Sam goaded me to try that stuff
And would not heed my strong rebuff
So finally he took the fork
Cut off a piece of emerald pork

He shoved that ham into his trap
To prove the green meat wasn't crap
Then spluttering to catch his breath
Sam-I-Am went to his death.

Until I learn what pathogen
Let Reaper show his wrath again
I shall avoid those eggs of green
I will avoid a tragic scene.

I will not eat them in a diner
Germs may dwell on the old china
I will not eat under hypnosis
I fear I will catch trichinosis

I will not eat them atop lettuce
The E. coli may upset us
I would not, could not, oh, the smell
I could not, would not, stinks like hell

I will not eat them with a gnu
I will not eat them in a stew
I will not eat them rare or often
I will not end up in a coffin

I'd rather dine on fish or fowl
or meat that comes from a mad cow
Green eggs and ham I will not eat
They were once safe—a salty treat!

But food-borne ills wait in our food
And so I'm just not in the mood.
I hope Sam's folks have clearly seen
That eating yolks of olive green
Is not a practice I would say
Is sanctioned by the FDA!

OK, OK, perhaps I'll try them
All things are tasty once you fry them
I'll try green eggs and ham, old Sam
I'll try them in my frying pan
Could it be I've been too cautious?
The worst case is I'll just be nauseous!

—The Grinch

GRINCH, 65

All the Whos down in Who-ville liked breakfast a bunch
And the Grinch,
Who lived just outside Who-ville,
Liked brunch!
The Grinch enjoyed brunches! From sausage to bacon!
He'd eat everything that the Who chefs were makin'.
He filled up his maw with the cooked and the raw
From oysters on ice to souffles without flaw!
But the Grinch made a flub,
That will keep this tale short.
The Grinch's decision
He could not abort.
A kid, Sam-I-Am, tempted him with some chow

That left the Grinch hospitalized until now
It seems that the green food consumed by this fella
Was laden—no crawling!—with live salmonella.
And what happened then?
Well, in Who-ville they say
That the Grinch's entrails
Spasmed three times that day!
He turned greener than normal, the shade of cooked peas
(Sam himself had croaked of this food-borne disease)
Prognosis was bleak, and he told his dog Max:
"I'm afraid that my judgment of people was lax."
Three thousand small Whos climbed up to Mount Crumpit
One brought a device for the stomach to pump it!
But the Grinch's large heart finally twinched its last twinch
So the Whos performed "You're a Dead One, Mr. Grinch!"

MRS. BUTTERWORTH TAKES SPILL

Sunday Breakfast Goes Terribly, Terribly Wrong

ST. PAUL, Minn. (AP) — A five-year-old girl was cited by authorities as being responsible for the catastrophic draining of Mrs. Butterworth at a local restaurant.

The tragedy occurred when the waitress at the You Betcha! Diner left the syrup on the table of a family that included two young daughters. Naturally, the girls immediately started touching things they were not supposed to, knocking over the venerable culinary icon.

Mrs. Butterworth's sweet, sticky essence hemorrhaged onto the table and down to the floor in seconds.

Unapologetic parents of the offending urchins explained that they encourage their children to "explore" the world in a self-directed manner. The manager of the You Betcha! requested that the family self-direct themselves out of the restaurant, never to return.

The empty Mrs. Butterworth was ceremoniously taped to the top of the cash register with a sign that reads "Curb Your Child."

ONCE UPON A TIME THERE WAS AN ENGINEER

Choo Choo Charlie, 35
Life Was Good But Not Plenty

DENVER (UPI) — A midlife crisis has made the tragic leap from pathetic to fatal. Choo Choo Charlie was killed in an accident as he pulled into the switching yard.

The National Transportation Safety Board cited operator error in the collision between Charlie's engine and an out-of-service caboose. Phone company logs show that the engineer recently started exchanging voluminous text messages with a woman identified only as "Sue." The content of the messages indicate that Sue is a younger woman who recently shook her caboose at Charlie. The engineer was texting at the time of the accident.

Charlie's wife said she knew something was up. "The bastard had just spent half of our retirement on a new sports car. Then he started working out, wearing nicer clothes, and was even trying a hair-restoration product."

An NTSB spokesman was asked whether the medications may have contributed to Charlie's downfall. He replied, "Charlie was definitely driving that train, high on Rogaine."

LITTLE ENGINE COULD; BRAKES COULD NOT

MILL VALLEY, Calif. (AP) — Children from five towns are making a pilgrimage to the scrap metal yard where pieces of the Little Engine lie in state. Just hours before, the Little Engine proved his mettle by pulling 17 carloads of food and toys destined for an orphanage over Pinnacle Mountain.

Six other Larger Engines refused the offer to make the delivery complaining that the load was too heavy. The Little Engine, a perky fellow who did light duty at the switching yard, was only slightly hesitant to take on the task, repeating to himself, "I have my doubts, I have my doubts."

Still, he decided he would try to help the starving children. As he passed the freight cars packed to the rafters with food, blankets, and toys destined for the starving, joyless children on the other side of the pass, he was heard to mutter, "I'm not so sure, I'm not so sure."

On a television in the depot, he saw motivational guru Tony Robbins exhorting the power of positive thinking, and he began puffing, "I just might do it, I just might do it."

At 11 a.m., hundreds of townspeople gathered at the switching yard, and many more lined the tracks up the mountainside to witness the event. Screams of "He's never going to make it!" and "Those kids will die!" were heard from the crowd.

As Little Engine puffed up Pinnacle Mountain, his steam-filled belly burned red-hot, and pouring all his might into the effort, he repeated his mantra, "I think I can, I think I can." Not a ringing self-endorsement but enough to push Little Engine over the peak with all 17 happy little freight cars in tow. Little Engine blew a great whistle to signal to townspeople that he'd made the near-vertical climb. He joyfully told himself, "I knew I could, I knew I could."

As he barreled down the mountainside toward the hungry, cold, toyless children at the depot, Little Engine suddenly realized his brakes could not handle such a heavy load at breakneck speeds.

One little boy who saw the engine and the 17 cars squeal past him in a blur of blue and red sparks heard the Little Engine cry, "I think I can stop! I think I can stop!"

THE NELL FENWICK INDEX:

Length of rope required to tie person to train tracks: 50 feet

Typical pounds of pressure required to break a human femur: 400 pounds

Typical weight of train locomotive: 400 tons

Number of pieces into which a person tied to tracks is sliced by a passing train: 4 (head, torso, legs)

Number of times Snidely Whiplash tied Nell to train tracks: 27

Number of times Dudley Do-Right saved Nell just in the nick of time: 26

Reverend Edward Haskell, 51, Dies by Own Hand

BUT DEATH IS RULED ACCIDENTAL

Eddie Haskel (right). Seen here with Wally Cleaver and unidentified girl.

WEST HOLLYWOOD, Calif. *(Los Angeles Times)* — Parishioners of the Third-Eye Church of the Righteous are mourning the loss of the Reverend Edward "Eddie Love" Haskell, 51. He was a strongly charismatic leader, beloved by members of his megachurch located in this bastion of sin, debauchery, and immorality. "Eddie Love" devoted much of his ministry in the last ten years to troubled young women between the ages of 20 and 35. His was the only church in Los Angeles County to have its own "baptismal" hot tub.

"He was so polite, so charming to everyone he met, especially the ladies," said an out-of-work actress and communicant of the church. "I don't know what it is, but he always had the right words for the right occasion. And what a head of hair."

The death was ruled an accident rather than suicide, as it appears Mr. Haskell was engaging in auto-erotic asphyxiation. Police found the victim wearing only a shirt, tie, and socks. A picture of Mrs. June Cleaver was on the floor nearby.

J. R. SHOT YET AGAIN!

Definitely Dead
No Need to Wait Until Fall Season To Learn Fate

DALLAS, Texas (UPI) — Billionaire oilman J. R. Ewing, 69, was found dead yesterday morning, splayed across the seat of his Lamborghini pickup truck, the victim of a gunshot wound. Ewing's pearl-handled Smith & Wesson sidearm was found by his side. In one hand, a copy of a personal bankruptcy statement; in the other, a bottle of Midori. A whisper campaign has begun among Southfork residents about how pathetic it was that Ewing, who had bought his way to the top of a liver transplant list, wasted his newly acquired organ on something other than bourbon.

Ewing's empire began to crumble with the collapse of Ewing Enterprises. He ran a bull semen Ponzi scheme, in which he convinced his own mother to invest. Miss Ellie lost everything and is down to her last head of cattle. To reduce expenses such as spousal support, J. R. got back together with his wife, giving her a case of genital herpes in the process.

Denizens of English betting parlors, who wagered heavily on Ewing's first gun injury in 1980 and again in 1991 when Ewing attempted suicide, were taken by surprise by this development in the family saga. The parlors are giving even odds on whether this is another dream sequence.

QUEEN OF HEARTS, 124, DIES

*Before All Those Death Sentences
Could Be Carried Out! Yippee!*

WONDERLAND (Reuters) — The acerbic
and domineering Queen of Hearts died today in Wonderland. The final cause of death
is unknown. For the past several weeks she
had been complaining of not feeling well
since having her own head cut off.

According to the White Rabbit, the body
can be viewed the day before tomorrow
starting at 4:00 p.m., and beginning promptly at 3:00 p.m. No one arriving before 5:00
p.m. will be admitted. The head can be
viewed the previous day.

Refreshments, a tray of tarts, will be served. Music at the service will be
performed by Grace Slick. Recently remarried, the Queen of Hearts is survived by her South African husband, the King of Diamonds, and a gay son,
the Jack of Clubs.

AFLAC DUCK KILLED IN BLAZE

BROWNSVILLE, Texas (UPI) — The AFLAC duck was braised today when an orange grove in which he was filming a commercial caught fire. The duck was promoting a new AFLAC insurance product aimed at the lucrative immigrant market. Members of a local armed militia are being questioned.

While the crew escaped safely, the frustrated, angry duck was caught in a thick glace of boiling fruit. He served six.

GEICO Spokesbrothers Killed

TOLLUND, Denmark (IPS) — GEICO spokesbrothers Caveman #1 and Caveman #2 were killed while filming one of their popular TV commercials. A temporary platform constructed for shooting collapsed, and the two cavemen fell into a bog. Officials plan to recover their bodies in 45,000 years.

Phil Connors, TV Weatherman Covering Groundhog Day, Killed by Chain Saw

PUNXSUTAWNEY, Pa. — Pittsburgh WPBH-TV9's popular weatherman, Phil Connors, was killed today as he attempted to juggle chain saws during his broadcast.

Connors, 43, explained to his audience that Groundhog Day was his most boring assignment of the entire year and that he planned to punch it up with the chain saws. Connor's producer, Rita Biberman, said Connors had not explained what he intended to do with the chain saws and had never been known to juggle before. She added, "He's always been a little unstable. He'll be sorely missed."

WPBH apologized to the Pittsburgh audience for the gruesome event and said it would require mental health evaluations for all future weather people.

Phil Connors, TV Weatherman Covering Groundhog Day, Killed by Bus

PUNXSUTAWNEY, Pa. — Pittsburgh WPBH-TV9's popular weatherman Phil Connors was killed today as he leaped in front of a bus, trying to save a 7-year-old boy. The boy, identified as Billy Miller, was also killed. Connors had just finished entertaining his television and live audiences with an impromptu chain saw-juggling exhibition, finishing to a huge applause.

Connors, 43, was covering the Punxsutawney Groundhog Day celebration for WPBH. Witnesses say he noticed the boy dart away from a group of friends and into the path of the oncoming bus. His producer, Rita Biberman, said Connors' reaction was instantaneous. "He didn't hesitate. He just ran across the fairgrounds. It was almost as if he started running toward the street before the boy. He'll be sorely missed."

Phil Connors, TV Weatherman Covering Groundhog Day, Killed by Food Poisoning

PUNXSUTAWNEY, Pa. — Pittsburgh WPBH-TV9's popular weatherman, Phil Connors, was killed today after sampling an assortment of local bratwurst during the Groundhog Day festival. Doctors at the Punxsutawney Medical and Feed Supply Center said some of the meat was not properly prepared, and there was nothing they could do to save him.

Earlier in the day, Connors had been a hero, saving the life of a local boy who had run in front of a bus. Con-

nors had come running from across the fairgrounds just in time to snatch Billy Miller out of the path of the on-coming vehicle.

Connors' producer, Rita Biberman, said the TV crew was in shock. "Phil was a great weatherman. He'd do anything to entertain his audience. After juggling chain saws and running in front of a bus, who would have thought the bratwurst was the most dangerous part of his day? He'll be sorely missed."

Phil Connors, TV Weatherman, and His Crew Killed in Highway Accident

PUNXSUTAWNEY, Pa. — Pittsburgh television station WPBH-TV9's popular weatherman, Phil Connors, was killed yesterday when his news van skidded off the highway just outside Punxsutawney. Connors, his producer, Rita Biberman, and his cameraman were all fatally injured and declared dead at the scene. Late last night, Mr. Connors and Ms. Biberman had announced their engagement.

Connors, 43, had been covering the Punxsutawney Groundhog Day celebration for WPBH. He had become a local

fan favorite and hero. In the course of one day, he had entertained the crowd with his masterful chain saw juggling and shortly thereafter saved a young boy from being hit by a bus. Later in the day, he was the host at the WPBH's festival booth, which was promoting "Proper Food-Handling Techniques."

Connors, apparently in a rush to return to Pittsburgh, had decided to make the trip despite white-out blizzard conditions. He had predicted a light dusting of snow. He will be sorely missed.

MARTY MCFLY

1968–1953

BELOVED SON
LOVING FATHER
OWN GRANDDAD

REGAN TERESA MacNEIL, 27

THE VATICAN (L'Osservatore Romano) — Regan MacNeil, a tourist from Washington, D.C., died last Tuesday when she accidentally fell into the Maderno fountain in St. Peter's Square.

Witnesses reported seeing MacNeil back into the holy water–filled fountain as she was taking pictures of the basilica. Several people reported seeing the woman's head spin 360 degrees after she fell into the holy fountain, which erupted into a furious boil. A nearby priest, reaching into the water to help her, was inexplicably sprayed from head to toe with what appeared to be pea soup.

No remains were found. The victim's family identified a 9-inch silver crucifix recovered from the fountain.

ADRIAN WOODHOUSE, 37

Rosemary's Only Baby

KILAUEA, Hawaii (*Wall Street Journal*) — Adrian Woodhouse, son of Rosemary and Guy Woodhouse of New York City, died last Friday while on a hiking trip in Hawaii when he fell into the active Kilauea volcano. Fellow hikers reported seeing Woodhouse walking extremely close to the mouth of the volcano and some said he appeared to have jumped. A park official commented that such a leap would be "like falling into the bowels of hell itself."

Mr. Woodhouse had a remarkable array of talents, excelling in a variety of fields. An attorney, scientist, as well as business and financial maven, his accomplishments included:

- Preparation of discovery defenses for R. J. Reynolds during tobacco litigation
- Manager of Enron pension plan
- Discovery of key processes for the development of genetically modified food
- A brief stint at second base for the Yankees
- Marriage counselor to Mary Matalin and James Carville
- Invented Pringles
- Played a mean fiddle
- Lead defense attorney for the Boston Archdiocese
- Longtime proponent of strip mining
- Life coach to Simon Cowell

Mr. Woodhouse died while on his honeymoon and is survived by his wife, Courtney Love.

Toddler Killed as Sailors Brawl

SANTA MONICA, Calif. (UPI) — A young child was killed today when he was left alone in a small boat that drifted in front of an oncoming freighter.

The child, named Swee'Pea, had boarded the boat as it was made ready by Popeye the Sailor Man. The police report states that an argument broke out between the father and a large bearded man regarding the paternity of the child. A fight ensued. During the altercation, the boat was released when one of the men pulled its pylon out of the water to strike the other man.

Horrified witnesses report that the men showed little interest in stopping the fight in order to save the child. In fact, some witnesses have charged that the sailor man actually stopped to have something to eat before attempting a rescue.

The child's mother was notified but was too skinny to comment.

ESTATE SALE— URGENT

SATURDAY, APRIL 4, 2 P.M.

Assets of Consummate Moocher Being Liquidated to Pay Off Hamburger IOUs

All items that belonged to the late J. Wellington Wimpy must be sold today to satisfy debts on Tuesday. Proceeds to fulfill probate court claims against Mr. Wimpy filed by the Rough House Café and four cardiologists owed money by Mr. Wimpy. Bidders must pay by certified check only—no credit will be extended.

PRODUCT RECALL: CRACKER JACKS TATTOO

SAN DIEGO (AP) — Inky Dinky Ink, Inc., has issued a voluntary recall of all rub-on tattoo prizes from boxes of Cracker Jacks because of possible contamination with the Hepatitis C virus.

The recall affects approximately 100 million boxes of the crunchy, delicious glazed popcorn and nuts. The FDA reports that the edible contents of the box are perfectly safe, but the tattoos are considered highly dangerous. One death has resulted from the tainted rub-on product: Sailor Jack, 26, who was on liberty in Thailand died shortly after he asked a young woman in a brothel to apply the tattoo to his arm with her spit.

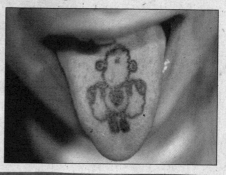

BAZOOKA JOE, 13

PHILADELPHIA (AP) — The Bureau of Alcohol, Tobacco, and Firearms is investigating the death of a boy who redeemed 20 million bubble gum comics for a rocket-propelled grenade launcher. The bubble gum maker hasn't a clue as to who fulfilled an order made by teenager Bazooka Joe. The toys offered as part of the redemption program are normally cheap plastic snap-togethers from China. It appears the RPG in question was made in Lithuania, and the FBI is investigating a Russian website where the comics were redeemed, called www.mikhailsnavy.com.

Police say this incident is unrelated to a case where two boys were able to order a Kalashnikov assault rifle from a Texas gun dealer in exchange for 5,000 Pokémon cards they had amassed. That weapon was intercepted before it was delivered.

The young Mr. Joe, apparently not realizing the grenade launcher was a shoulder-fired weapon, shot it like a tommy gun. The recoil popped his head like a bubble.

A spokesman for the National Rifle Association said this episode, like Mr. Joe's comic strips, is not a laughing matter. "Bazooka Joe should have known better. He lost an eye when playing with a toy version of a bazooka he got in the mail for 400 gum comics in 1967. RPGs are another matter. We always recommend that young people who use weapons, whether or not they are legally acquired, practice extreme caution when discharging them."

Consumer safety groups are still recoiling from the NRA's pronouncement.

Local Cleaning Girl Found Dead in the Road

Covered with Blood and Pumpkin

NEUSCHWANSTEIN, Germany (*Medieval Reporter*) — The county sheriff's office reported the gruesome discovery of a woman's body last night in the middle of Castle Road. She was discovered by partygoers returning from the Prince's ball.

The body was identified as that of Cinderella, a cleaning girl and stepchild to a local family. The cause of death appeared to be blunt trauma from the road, as if she had fallen from a speeding coach.

The cinder girl was shoeless, and her feet were badly cut by broken crystal found on the road. The sheriff had no explanation for why the body was covered with pumpkin. The coroner put the time of death at 12:01 a.m.

48

Blind and Bitter, Cinderella's Stepsisters Die at Palatial Home; Life of Riches, Excess, and Ugliness

VILLAGERS WONDER: CAN WE RAID THEIR CLOSETS?

THE KINGDOM (*Daily Realm Express*) — Their accomplishments were few, their friends fewer, and their good deeds nil. Birds gouged out their eyes for their wickedness and falsehoods. They most certainly had no sex in the city in a pair of Manolo Blahniks, having cut off their toes in an attempt to fit into a famous glass slipper. It goes without saying that *Fairyland's Next Top Model* wasn't beating down their door. And now, the most infamous stepsisters in the Kingdom are dead.

Their father reports that the hateful duo spitefully shoved Cinderella's godmother into the fireplace during a recent visit. What they didn't realize was that the old woman was a magical fairy who would, with the final flick of a wand, turn them into piles of pig manure. The Eastern mystics refer to this circumstance as karma, loosely translated as "Payback's a bitch."

At this time of sadness, the gentry can think of only one thing: "Who is going to get their fashion-forward clothing collection?" It's to die for! The fugly siblings famously owned the most awe-inspiring stockpile of ball gowns and tiaras in the realm! And word is that their ready-to-wear pieces, purchased in Milan, would make the Queen jealous.

NOTE: The obituary editor for the Daily Realm Express declined a request to write about Cinderella's wretched stepsisters, so it fell to the style editor. The Sunday Daily Realm will carry full coverage of the runway showing of their couture collection during Post Mortem Fashion Week.

Runway commentary will be provided by snarky experts from Maison Rumpelstiltskin and Vogue.

SNOW WHITE, 59

Who's the Deadest One of All?

THE BLACK FOREST (Reuters) — According to a reliable Looking Glass, Snow White has unhappily entered the "ever after." After liberation from a glass coffin, she lived a "charmed" life in a gated community.

Filled with nostalgia, White returned to the forest home of her youth that she shared with seven jolly but messy miners. She discovered that the now-elderly dwarfs were in need of 24-hour attention. As queen, White had rejected universal health care for her subjects, provoking criticism that she was not the fairest one of all.

Her karmic reward? Instead of one grumpy dwarf, she now had to take care of seven. The bedpans. The cigar ashes. Piles of dirty dishes. And no more squirrels or birds to provide free labor. White toiled all day, and she wasn't exactly whistling while she worked. Her nights? Insurance forms. The last straw was the letter from the HMO denying benefits for seven cases of black lung.

She went to the cupboard and took a bite of an apple she had been saving.

'Snow More!'

Help Wanted

Live-in nursing care professional for seven elderly dwarfs. Room and board included.

Experience with range of temperaments, illnesses, and disabilities preferred. Position includes colorful uniform with inexplicably high collar.

TOOTH FAIRY (577–2004)

SHENANDOAH, W. Va. (UPI) — Phil Gold, publicist and spokesman for the Tooth Fairy, announced that she died suddenly last Saturday while in the line of duty. She was 1,427.

Miss Fairy was collecting teeth on November 5 following a particularly successful Halloween for the children of West Virginia. Traveling in heavy fog with a large load, she flew into the side of the Appalachian Mountains. The NTSB classified the cause of the accident as "pixie error."

In the wake of the Tooth Fairy's demise, Gold says that children should flush lost teeth down the toilet and ask their parents for a dollar.

TRIBUNE CLASSIFIEDS

Now Hiring! Work your own hours, travel widely, earn air miles; great job for compulsive hoarder. Dental hygienists given first priority. Ability to tiptoe quietly through bedrooms a plus but not necessary—will train. Experience handling petty cash. Position open immediately! Contact Mayor of Fairy Land: 415-555-3444.

LOST AND FOUND

Found: Handsome but dead frog stuck to bottom of wagon wheel. Dressed in charming outfit of velvet, sequins, and tiny crown. Discovered yards away from princess slumbering in glass coffin. Missing a pet? Contact Lord Farqaad, castle on the hill.

SANDMAN DEAD

Don't Lose Any Sleep Over It

SLEEPY HOLLOW, N.Y. (UPI) — The Sandman, a hallowed figure in the establishment of proper slumber habits and dream production, has taken a permanent leave of absence from consciousness.

Mr. Sandman was a celebrated world traveler and kept an apartment in Sleepy Hollow. The magical dust he poured in children's eyes was intended to bring good dreams.

Pharmaceutical lobbyists claimed that the multi-billion-dollar insomnia industry would be at great risk if Sandman were allowed to continue his unregulated practices. Mr. Sandman vehemently defended his sleep-induction method as time-tested and harmless. But big pharma prevailed. The FDA issued a statement advising that clinical trials have yet to be performed on sand as a sleep aid. The Center for Disease Control warned of mini-epidemics of conjunctivitis, or "pinkeye," and issued an orange level warning to cover all windows with duct tape and plastic until further notice.

Dr. Sanjay Gupta came out against him. Nancy Grace did an exposé. He went on *The View*, and for the first time Whoopi Goldberg and Elisabeth Hasselback agreed on something—they hated him. Things got worse when he did an interview and was sandbagged by Larry King.

A dejected Mr. Sandman went back to his hotel room, put the "Do Not Disturb" sign on his door, tucked himself into bed and died in his sleep.

FDA GRAS* ALTERNATIVES TO SANDMAN:

1. Glass of milk
2. Poetry collection
3. Jimmy Kimmel
4. Turkey dinner
5. Sheep counting
6. Lullabies
7. Nip of Old Grand Dad
8. White noise machine from Sharper Image
9. Chamomile tea
10. Ambien for Kidz®

(*Generally Recognized as Safe, but seek advice from professionals before reading poetry, serving milk, or dispensing lullabies.)

MAN ON THE STREET

Q: What is the worst thing you have hit with your car?

A: "I saw a flickering light, then it hit the windshield like an ostrich egg. I tried putting on the wipers, but it smeared even more. After the accident, I didn't have the heart to tell the children what happened. Later that night, I scraped Tinkerbell off and buried her in the garden."

—Roger Nottingly, father of four, who think their dad can do no wrong

MAN ON THE STREET

Q: What is the worst thing you have hit with your car?

A: "Blimey! That would have to be Austin Powers. Chrissakes, how was I to know he'd be leading a marching band full of beautiful women down the middle of a busy London street?"

—Taxi driver Billy Shears, on trial for involuntary manslaughter

Pat the Bunny, 68

ST. FRANCIS ANIMAL HOSPITAL, N.Y. (AP) — Pat the Bunny, soft and fluffy subject of stroking by millions of cooing infants, has died following a long illness.

Pat contracted *alopecia leporidae*, a rare condition resulting in the shedding of all her hair. It was caused by repeated applications of baby drool. Pat's market share dropped dramatically when her mangy appearance repulsed legions of hyper-cautious, germ-wary parents.

Rivals soon moved to fill the void left by the spurned bunny, including Sniff the Fox, Flick the Gnat, and Squash the Ferret. Needless to say, nothing ever came close to the tactile sensation one received from Pat. Even animal rights activists found her pliant pelt oddly comforting.

Toward the end, Pat was in the care of the Quiet Old Lady who whispers "Hush" and reportedly said good night to the hair brush, mirror, a dress, a bowlful of mush, and the moon before gently falling into permanent slumber. Good night, Pat!

Breakfast Brawl Bumps Off Beloved Bunnies

FIGHT OVER WHETHER TRIX REALLY ARE FOR KIDS; POLICE THWARTED BY SLIPPERY MIXTURE OF CEREAL AND FLAVORED MILK

CONEY ISLAND, N.Y. (AP) — It was supposed to be a meeting of the minds. Two celebrity spokesbunnies and their entourages arrived at this run-down resort area to talk sugar, milk, and fame. An audience of 300 early-childhood development experts were present for a discussion of marketing strategies and their relation to proper nutrition. This would be the first-ever meeting of the Nesquik Bunny and Silly Rabbit. And it would not end well.

The pellets hit the fan when they sat down for breakfast and Quiky made a derisive remark about the colorful bowls of cereal in front of them. A reporter caught the exchange on tape:

Silly Rabbit: "What did you say?"

Nesquik Bunny: "I said, 'Trix are not for us,' man. Dig—this stuff is full of artificial colors and flavors, and we rabbits got a lot of reproducin' to do. We can't be fillin' our bodies with this junk!"

Silly: "And is strawberry milk any better?"

Nesquik: "No, but I never said my drink was for rabbits. We're herbivores. This stuff we're pushin' on TV is for kids—for kids, man."

That was it. If Silly had heard it once, he'd heard it a thousand times. Out came the spoons. Bodyguards couldn't pull them apart. There was much pulling of ears, gnashing of unusually long front teeth, and bouncing off walls. When police arrived, it was too late—fur and colorful balls of cereal littered the hall, and traumatized conference goers were covered in flavored milk.

Silly leaves behind 123,566 offspring; Nesquik, 10,940. And it is likely that, after this incident, not a single one of their progeny will be able to even look at a bowl of Trix without thinking of this tragic day. So, kids, go ahead and eat up. Trix are for you. And only for you.

𝔄 Resolution

Whereas: Mermaids are a beloved part of our culture and sea life; and

Whereas: The killing of mermaids is known to bring bad luck to those societies that cause it; and

Whereas: Sea Nymph is not a recognized sandwich meat; and

Whereas: No child should be forced to discover bits of one of their favorite water sprite in their lunch box; and

Whereas: One Sally Benson of Cedar Junction, Iowa, did just that and to this day still has nightmares of red hair and green tail in all her food.

Be It Resolved that this legislative body will develop, submit, and pass legislation supporting the clear labeling and marketing of "Mermaid-Safe Tuna."

Fishermen Discover Entire Undersea Village Wiped Out From Toxins

Sub Recovers Bizarre Bodies, Including Square Sponge with Pants

BIKINI BOTTOM (UPI) — Autopsies have been performed on several grotesque creatures recovered from the Pacific Ocean floor, 1,000 miles west of San Diego. A Navy submersible was sent to this remote location after fishermen pulled up a hollowed-out pineapple with tiny furniture in it.

The undersea village, complete with movie theater and restaurants, appeared to be deserted, until researchers steered their sub toward the Krusty Krab restaurant. Inside were the bodies of creatures heretofore unknown to marine biologists: a bloated purple starfish, a two-eyed octopus with a frightening noselike growth, a hideously rotund crab in blue jeans, and, most curiously, a square yellow sponge with bulgy eyes, a necktie, and pants. All appeared to have been feeding on a burgerlike substance.

Tests confirm that a key ingredient in the Krabby Patties is crab liver, or tomalley, which can amass high levels of neurotoxins when there is a Yellow Tide. Scientists advise eating Krabby Patties only during months ending in "g."

Farmer Had Dog

There was a farmer who had a dog and Bingo was his name-o
T-I-C-K-S
F-L-E-A-S
M-I-T-E-S
and Bingo was his name-o.

There was a farmer who had a dog and Bingo was his name-o
M-A-N-G-E
W-O-R-M-S
P-A-R-V-O
and Bingo was his name-o.

There was a farmer who had a dog and Bingo was his name-o
R-A-B-I-E (s)
C-O-U-G-H
C-R-A-M-P
and Bingo was his name-o.

There was a farmer who had a dog and Bingo was his name-o
A-T-O-P-Y
T-U-M-O-R
B-L-O-A-T
and Bingo was his name-o.

There was a farmer who had a dog and Bingo was his name-o
N-O-D-E-S
F-E-V-E-R
T-R-U-C-K
and Bingo was his name-o.

MISS MARY MACK, 14

Girl Scouts Worldwide Mourn Tragic Death following Improvised Lyrics to Clapping Game

Miss Mary Mack, Mack, Mack
All dressed in black, black, black
With silver buttons, buttons, buttons
All down her back, back, back.

She asked her mother, mother, mother
For 50 cents, cents, cents
To see the elephants, elephants, elephants
Jump over the fence, fence, fence.

They jumped so high, high, high
They reached the sky, sky, sky
And landed back, back, back,
On Miss Mary Mack, Mack, Mack.

ATTORNEY: "IMPOSTORS" ATTEMPT TO LAY CLAIM TO ESTATE OF FAMED NOBODY

347,000 Former Summer Campers Testify to Being the Real John Jacob Jingleheimer Schmidt

---

Probate Court Erupts in Repetitive Repetitive Song; Session Lasts For Hours

Papa Bear Pleads Self-Defense in Slaying of Golden-Haired Intruder

WESTPHALIA (Reuters) — Black Forest resident Helmut Urso was being held in lieu of $100 cash bail for the mauling death of an alleged burglar, according to Westphalia Police. Urso, his wife, and son arrived home Tuesday to find their lunch partially eaten, a broken chair, and their beds in disarray.

The intruder, who was awakened by the bears, reportedly rushed toward them wielding a heavy picnic basket. Mrs. Urso was beaten about the face, hands, and chest. Papa Bear stopped the assault by tearing the attacker to pieces.

The bears had entered the cottage with much trepidation because a rash of home invasions by wolves, separate incidents that resulted in the deaths of a kindly old grandmother and three little pigs. A wolf recently killed a shepherd boy when local villagers refused to respond to his numerous calls for help. With the door to their home wide open and porridge spilled all over the floor, the bears were concerned.

Police are piecing together the evidence and the victim. Forensics investigators have recovered several locks of golden hair, a blue dress, a white bodice, and a tibula. Anyone who knows an individual fitting this description is asked to phone Westphalia police.

Mama Bear is being treated at Thumbelina Memorial Hospital with hot salt baths. Papa Bear is cooling off in a jail cell. Baby Bear is "just right."

Della Young, 24,
James Dillingham Young, 26

Magi Were Really, Really Stingy This Time

NEW YORK (AP) — Della Young, whose formerly long, lush hair used to be admired by neighbors in her tenement building, and James Young, the bright young draftsman, were found dead in their apartment, victims of exposure.

A neighbor, William Porter, said the Youngs were the victims of circumstances starting four Christmases ago when Della sold her hair to buy Jim a chain for his beloved pocket watch, while Jim simultaneously sold his pocket watch to buy tortoise shell combs for Della's fulsome hair.

The next Christmas, Jim sold his drafting table to buy Della a mother-of-pearl toothbrush. Unbeknown to him, she had her teeth pulled and used the gold fillings to buy him a compass and caliper.

After the couple had a child, Della sold the baby to gypsies to buy Jim a beer-brewing kit. The same morning, he sold a kidney to buy his wife a pram buggy so she could stroll the child proudly throughout the neighborhood.

Glaucoma sufferer Jim sold his eyeglasses to buy Della a pair of garnet earrings for her birthday. To celebrate his promotion to church deacon, Della sold her unusually beautiful ears to a medical school for anatomy study and used the proceeds to buy Jim a miniature bible.

Sadly, or perhaps not so, this would be the last Christmas for the Young couple.

A local pawnshop owner told the *Sun* that on Christmas Eve, Jim hocked all his clothes to buy Della a gold-plated patented fire starter. On that freezing cold morning, Della sold every lump of coal from the Youngs' winter storage bin to buy her husband a cedar chest for his woolens.

RECENT DEATHS

Old Woman, 67—Single mother. Lived in shoe. Passed away from exhaustion and despair, with shoelace around neck, at home. Leaves 19 children, 4 dogs, and 2 parakeets. Burial will be in spacious shoebox.

Will Shoemaker, 77—General contractor. Expanded Old Woman's shoe to hipboot; flip-flopped after fathering 19 children and left Old Woman for young woman in set of red pumps. Died while constructing 25,000-room museum to house Imelda Marcos collection.

Arthur Paddywack, 50—Old man. Had a knack for nicking bones to feed to strays. Bitten by mad dog while playing a fetching game called Seven. Has gone to heaven.

Chicken Little, 27—Demogogue. Died when giant video screen fell on her head as she gave rousing speech to thousands at rally about dangers of free-ranging.

Children of Old Woman Who Lived in a Shoe Write Tell-All Memoir

WEST SUSSEX (*County Times*) — Nineteen members of a shoe-dwelling family have published a shocking memoir, rife with tales of starvation and abuse. *We Didn't Know What To Do Either!* chronicles the lives of wretched siblings forced to squeeze out a meager existence on a shoestring.

"Now that the ol' woman is in the ground, our story can be told," Neville Aston, son #4, said. The book contains a dramatic account of an incident when the children were fed broth and no bread, whipped soundly, and put to bed.

"Well, it wasn't bad broth really," admitted Maggie Aston, daughter #10. "But who would read a memoir these days if it was just a bunch of rot about how Mum was house proud and knitted afghans and served tea promptly at 5? It's like our agent told us—scandal sells."

Old Mother Hubbard, a member of the organization Single Moms Attempting to Cope with Kids (SMACK), came to the little old woman's defense. "Those ungrateful little urchins! She was a single parent living in a bloody shoe with 19 screaming kids. If they were mine, they would have gotten that shoe right up their collective bum!"

Jack, Beanstalk Baron, 86

COUNTY KERRY, Ireland (AP) — Old age has taken the life of Jack, who lived in a legendary home in the clouds on Carrantuohill, Ireland's highest peak.

Impoverished at birth, Jack gained vast wealth with the acquisition of a golden-egg-laying goose. Unfortunately for the population of his birthplace, Durham, England, Jack incurred the wrath of a Giant for stealing the goose. The colossal, angry leviathan chased Jack down a flimsy beanstalk, lost his grip, and hurtled down onto the town, flattening 1,487 residents, 419 homes, and hundreds of livestock. The beanstalk never yielded a single bean.

Jack and his mother paid out settlements to afflicted families and fled their decrepit shack in Durham to set up housekeeping in a newly built castle on Carrantuohill, nicknamed "Fee Fi Fo Farm."

There, he carefully guarded his goose, bought and sold land, foreclosed on widows, and reportedly took a liking to bone pudding.

JULY 24, 1967

Candlestick Jumper's Risky Hobby Proves Fatal

SALT LAKE CITY (AP) — Here under the flat roof of the Peaks Ice Arena and out of the scrutiny of the media, Jack Bernard Nimble spent three hours a day practicing what he hoped would soon be the latest sensation in winter sports: extreme candlestick jumping. The sport involves skating at a high velocity and making a broad jump over a tall set of candlesticks, with hopes of landing on one's skates on the other side.

Nimble had planned to unveil his two newest jumps at the 1967 U.S. Candlestick Jumping Championships in Houston, Texas, with President Johnson in attendance. But the jumper's hopes went up in flames when he, himself, went up in flames. Nimble's coach, Evel Knievel, said that he and Jack had been out the night before at Chubby's Chili Bowl downing crocks of Seven Bean Mean Chili and beer.

Jack had safely cleared the "Menacing Menorah," a line of eight giant flames, and the daredevil was attempting an audacious "Liberace" maneuver (a flamboyantly flaming candelabra that produces 100,000 BTUs) when the catastrophe occurred. The skin-tight costume he was wearing had filled to capacity with chili-induced methane, and a not-so-quick Nimble vaporized in a flash of brilliant blue light.

The Rolling Stones are reportedly writing a paean to the jumper for their next album.

Florida Contractor Who Jacked Clients is Jacked Himself

DELRAY BEACH, Fla. (UPI) — This was the house that Jack built. But now, the house and its contents are nothing but a pile of rubble. Residents in this growing city of 142,000 are stunned by the implosion that took place just blocks from their own homes, which were built by Jack's development company, Jack's Development Company. Most of the homes were bought, sight unseen, and flipped for a profit by out-of-state speculators during the housing boom. Poor craftsmanship, cheap materials, and an utter lack of engineering prowess doomed Jack's own house to failure.

The crooked man who built a crooked house is now buried under a crooked pile of debris. The building commissioner is now reviewing all the homes that Jack built in the past five years and issued this statement from the scene:

"This is the roof that's made of wood
That landed on Jack while eating his food
That he put on his table by cheating the good
Who trusted Jack to be a man of his word
But were bilked when the contractor lured
Them into trusting him to build
McMansions
That caused a shock
That stopped a clock
That didn't chime
But told the time
Of the end of the house that Jack built."

TWINKLING LITTLE STAR EXPLODES IN SUPERNOVA; SCIENTISTS NO LONGER WONDER WHAT IT IS

(see page 14)

CORRECTION

On Tuesday, Oct. 22, we reported that the county coroner had concluded that the cause of death of Miss Penelope Muffet, 16, resulted from the consumption of tainted curds. However, it appears that the Bristol native died from a previously undiagnosed case of coronary arrhythmia, complicated by severe arachnophobia.

—Editor

COW, 23

Gravity Takes Life of 1,025-Pound Mother of 17

Bovine Achieved World Record High Jump, Lacked Plan for Return Trip

HASTINGS, Neb. (AP) — A local cow made history by jumping over the moon last night, only to come crashing down at 32 feet per second. The town of Hastings will honor the accomplishment with a barbecue on Saturday.

Pepper Picker/ Processor Piper Perishes in Prison

BY PENELOPE PRICHARD-PARSONS

PETALUMA, Pa. (*Petaluma Press*) — Peter Piper, picker and professional pickler of peppers, has passed on peacefully in prison.

Prior to a period at the penitentiary, Piper possessed partnership in a pickling plant. Poor pay practices put public pressure on Piper, who portrayed the paltry pecks of peppers picked by produce personnel as "pathetic for profits."

A plethora of persistent public prosecutors piled petty, pointless plaints on Peter. Police say Piper presented payment to prosecutors for preferential protection. "Petulant perpetrator!" pettifoggers pressed potently.

Perspicacious pals passionately protested Piper's persecution. Pointless was the polyphony of pleas, as precipitous pillories proved piercingly poisonous. Prevaricating, pathos-piqued Peter pleaded for pity.

Prudence prohibited prosecutorial progressiveness, provoking punctilious punishment.

Prison propagated putrefaction in Piper's political posture, profoundly preying on Peter's perception of plunderous Plutocracies. Poise prevailed, putting plaintive Piper at peace with pernickety persecutors.

HATTIE MAY SNELL, 82

CRIPPLED WIDOW KILLED BY BOARDERS SHE SAVED FROM STARVATION

HAD RECENTLY FINISHED BUILDING FANCIFUL HOME COVERED IN BREAD AND SWEETS

BLACK FOREST (Reuters) — Kindly and generous, always with a twinkle in her eye, Hattie May Snell was memorialized by friends and neighbors at a midnight magic circle during the latest full moon.

Two young thieves reduced Snell, 82, to a pile of ashes in her own oven; they also robbed the widow of her earthly possessions. It was the very oven she used to bake sugar cookie shingles for her home, sweets used to help save the lives of lost and starving children.

For weeks, the ungrateful kids gorged on Ms. Snell's home-baked home, and it is believed she was just about to send them back to their ramshackle abode when they turned on her.

"Those two delinquents set out to create terror and mischief: double, double, toil, and trouble!" Hattie's sister Valkyrie lamented. Others in the coven agreed that the duo is trying to get away with murder: "Fair is foul, and foul is fair," said one of the attendees. "Parties burn and nonsense bubble," said another.

Motive for the crime against Sister Snell appears to be robbery. The father of the accused, a poor woodcutter, had recently reported the acquisition of a great fortune, the provenance of which is unknown. The Imperial Revenue Service is investigating. If apprehended, alleged murderers Hansel and Gretel will be tried as adults because they are so plump and potentially delicious.

Wayne Szalinski's Latest Documentary Chronicles Tragic Death of His Children:

"HONEY, I CRUSHED THE KIDS"

WTF HAPPENED TO ROY G. BIV?

Untimely Death Causes Abbreviated Vacation

WPB, Fla. (MSNBC) — SOHO resident and Rainbow Coalition member ROY G. BIV was on VACA in FLA from his job with UNICEF. BIV had been getting some R&R visiting EPCOT, NASA, and had a VIP pass to the big race courtesy of NASCAR. BIV was SCUBA diving. Although PADI certified, he seems to have panicked after an equipment SNAFU. Things became FUBAR PDQ and then he was SOL. The dive master missed BIV's SOS. When he wasn't back by his ETA, the crew went looking for him ASAP, which was SOP. The captain searched, "hoping he'd be A-OK. When we found him, I thought, OMG! This SOB has made his MILF a widow!" He was rushed to a local ER where an MD pronounced him DOA.

RIP, ROY G. BIV.

BLUE, 64

EVEN CRAYONS GET THE BLUES

BURNT SIENNA, Ore. — The Crayola 64 box has an empty slot tonight after the passing of one of everyone's favorite crayons, Cerulean.

Cerulean, known by his friends simply as "Blue," was rushing between assignments when he stopped to have lunch in his car. The exhausted paraffin stick fell asleep in the hot sun with the windows closed and melted into a pool of pigment.

Several of the other crayons were angry and claim that overwork led to the death.

One pastel who wished to remain anonymous explained: "It's too much. Blue was up at 5:00 a.m. painting a one-sided house for a boy in Cedar Rapids. Do you think the kid wanted to use a few different colors? No! Monochromatic. Cerulean had to do the whole job."

"After that he rushed over to a gig at the George S. Patton Montessori Nursery School where Malcolm Hoover was doing a landscape with a 2-inch-high tree and a 9 ½-inch Cerulean sky! Which, I might add, he colored in twice!"

"You'd think he'd get a break, but, no! It was on to Des Moines, where David Carson was doing a Jackson Pollack on his mother's living room wall. Blue was the central theme. It was 3 feet high and 8 feet long. They worked him like a PENCIL!"

Some of the crayons blame the suits at Crayola. Neon Carrot was one of the few crayons willing to speak out. "What kills us is the sharpener. Every time kids realize how badly they draw, what's the first thing they do? Reach for the sharpener! Peel, sharpen. Sharpen, peel. They should outlaw those things! But, instead, they put one right on the back of the box!"

Crayola has announced they are bringing the old veteran Blue Gray out of retirement while they search for Cerulean's permanent replacement.

WHERE IS WALDO?

Search Ends on Remote Pacific Island, and News is Not Good

YAFUFLA, New Guinea (AP) — Family and friends of 25-year-old world traveler Waldo, famous for blending into crowds wherever he goes, report he has "blended in" for good in a village in southeastern Papua, New Guinea.

Following the GPS coordinates in Waldo's cell phone, searchers were led to lands occupied by the Korowai people, one of the world's last-surviving tribes of cannibals.

Apparently, Waldo's trademark glasses, striped sweater, and woolen cap caused him to stand out among the grass-skirted villagers as a particularly delicious-looking morsel.

Officials say the recovery of girl-friend Wenda and dog Woof may also occur in the next three days, depending on the digestive systems of the Korowai.

Thurston Howell IV, 38, Dies of Privilege

BRUSSELS (AP) — Bon vivant heir to the Howell Industries fortune, Thurston Howell IV, has collapsed at a dinner party from bingeing on Dark and Stormies. The son of Thurston Howell III and his wife, Lovey, "Thirsty" the Fourth apparently spent the last of his inheritance by flying across the Atlantic and buying Europe a drink.

Thirsty had his mother and father declared dead four hours after they failed to return from a tour aboard the S.S. *Minnow*.

After receiving a phone call from a Singaporean girlfriend who told him that she was about to have Thurston Howell V, Thirsty decamped to Spain, where he began a $300,000 tour of bars and pubs, guaranteeing that the last scion of the Howell family would not inherit a dime.

Thirsty Howell IV will be buried on a remote island, the remaining asset from the formerly vast holdings of Howell Industries, three hours by boat from Hawaii.

Remains of Bridge Troll Found Scattered on Cascade; Three Gruff Billy Goats Held for Questioning

BERGEN, Norway (UPI) — Police are hoping that the scene they came upon recently will only happen "once upon a time" and never again. After hill-dwellers complained of a foul stench coming from an area near Svendson's Bridge, investigators discovered a landscape littered with the rotting corpse of a troll (which isn't much different from the smell of a living troll).

Dozens of turkey vultures were feasting on the remains of Torbjorn Johansen, a hermitic fellow who lived beneath the bridge in a small hovel of his own making. The puzzling scene, of a 600-pound hunchback broken into hundreds of pieces with his eyes gouged out, has caused police to suspect foul play. Johansen's voluminous personal journals provide no evidence of known enemies of the sometimes-cranky troll. Estranged family members said Johansen was often very protective of his bridge and made empty threats toward those who passed over it without his permission.

Three rather uncooperative and brash billy goats are being held for questioning. The fattest of the three was said to have blood on his horns that matched that of the victim.

The bridge is now being patrolled by a local garden gnome.

74

CHEWBACCA, MERCENARY FOR REBEL ALLIANCE, DEAD AT 47 (329 IN HUMAN YEARS)

WALES (IPS) — Mr. Chewbacca, known to his friends as Chewie, died yesterday. He was best known as first mate of Han Solo's ship, the *Millennium Falcon*. He fought with distinction during the war with the Galactic Empire and was famously snubbed, undecorated during the medals ceremony following the Rebel victory.

Chewbacca attended Obedience School at Phillips-Andover where he excelled at Ultimate Frisbee.

Born on the planet Monoxidyl, Chewbacca had once been saved by Han Solo and joined him in service of his Life Debt. Having saved Solo's life during the Empire wars, Chewbacca was released of his Life Debt and retired to Earth. He enjoyed anonymity in Greece, where, lounging at the beach in his Speedo, he blended in with the locals.

Tiring of Greece, Chewbacca embarked on a trip through Europe. He was welcomed as a hero across the continent, but his reception in England was less than cordial. Having fallen behind on his rabies vaccination, English law required that he spend six months in quarantine. During that time, he came down with a honking case of kennel cough and died a few weeks later.

Mr. Chewbacca will be stuffed and mounted with full military honors and put on display at the Westminster Kennel Club through July.

Simba

Serengeti, June 15, 2011
Remington Bolt Action Rifle Model 700 SPS SS 300 WSM
Elmer J. Fudd

MARY POPPINS, 70

Governess, Counselor, RAF Colonel

LONDON (*Daily Telegraph*) — A popular governess rumored to have magical powers, Mary Poppins was killed on Sunday when an umbrella she was flying crashed into Covent Garden.

She was 70.

Air traffic controllers at Heathrow Airport had received a mayday message from the airborne nanny shortly before the crash. Ms. Poppins was an active member of the Home Office Bumbershoot Brigade, an elite wing of flying au pairs tasked with supporting antiterrorist activities. She had been monitoring the annual Pakistan versus England Kite Fighting match in Hyde Park.

The Air Safety Board has recovered the umbrella's flight data recorder. A preliminary review shows that the main flight control system had suffered a supercalifragilisticexpialidocious failure immediately before the crash.

In lieu of burial, the Church of England has commissioned a three-dimensional chalk mausoleum to be drawn around the body by Poppins's friend Bert.

Lead Singer for Chipmunks Found Dead in Hotel Room

FRONT MAN ALVIN HAD HISTORY OF ADDICTION
HOTEL BED COVERED WITH ACORNS
CORONER IDENTIFIES VICTIM BY LACK OF TWO FRONT TEETH

Jane and Michael Banks: Poppins "Meaner, Nastier, Crueler" than Portrayed in Popular Movie

LONDON (*Daily Telegraph*) — Brother and sister Jane and Michael Banks reacted to the death of their former nanny, Mary Poppins, with great relief. At a press conference outside their home in London, the now-grown Banks siblings explained that Poppins "muddled their minds" to the point that they became paranoid social misfits.

"Poppins dragged us to freaky places. She had a mad uncle who floated in the air near the ceiling. An old lady friend at a candy shop who snapped off her fingers and told us they were 'gingerbread'! Oh, and she loved this filthy bloke who lived in the park and had the fakest Cockney accent we've ever heard. We told our parents about these so-called 'adventures.' Poppins denied they ever happened and called us bratty little liars," said the withdrawn and pallid Jane Banks.

Michael Banks was similarly emphatic. "She could talk to animals! The woman came and went with the wind! On an umbrella, no less! You do believe us, don't you?" cried the whey-faced, balding actuarial. "Poppins was still showing up out of nowhere up 'til last week, made us clean our rooms, and force-fed us teaspoons of 'medicine'!"

This reporter asked if the vagabond nanny administered the medication in a most delightful way.

"You mean with a spoonful of sugar? Rubbish! It was bitter and made us hallucinate! I've still got a headache."

In the 1950s, Mary Poppins' popular memoir was adapted for the screen by Disney, which this reporter pointed out to the spluttering Ms. Banks. "Which is a good reason to bring back book-burning," exclaimed the former librarian. With that, the wan siblings closed and locked the door to their apartment and closed the shades.

Dinosaur Operator Killed at Stone Quarry

BEDROCK — A crane engineer was killed at Slate Rock & Gravel Company last Tuesday when he fell from the Brontosaurus he was operating.

Fred Flintstone, a twelve-year veteran, died from injuries suffered from landing on a pile of rocks while dismounting from his bronto. Mr. Slate, president of Slate Rock & Gravel, claims the blame lies squarely with Flintstone, who insisted on surfing off the tail of his bronto in clear violation of company policy. Crane and Rig union officials have filed a grievance. A hearing is scheduled for Friday.

Flintstone's widow, Wilma, has retained the services of attorney Perry Masonite.

Extinction Claims Barney, the Purple Dinosaur

LAS COLINAS, Texas (AP) — Barney the Purple Dinosaur is history.

Star of his own PBS television series and Broadway-style spectaculars, Barney's message of unbridled joy and carefree optimism annoyed millions of adults. But parents tolerated the gleeful biped because of his skill at reducing toddlers to a post-hypnotic state, which increased moms and dads' chance of getting the laundry done in peace.

Barney's life's work represented the most successful collaboration between humans and dinosaurs since *Land of the Lost*. The purple Tyrannosaurus became extinct on Wednesday in a freak accident. While filming a sequence for his show, a giant inflatable "meteor" dropped from the stage's rafters and knocked Barney into a kiddie pool filled with green slime. The crew worked furiously to free him from the muck by pulling on Barney's sneakers but failed. Time and tide would seal the dinosaur's fate.

A memorial service will be held in Provincetown, Mass., at the cottage Barney shared with longtime friend Tinky Winky.

After a round of "I Love You, You Love Me," his remains will be merrily deposited in the La Brea tar pits.

CRUELLA DE VIL, 66

LOVED NICKNAMES GIVEN BY BRITISH TABLOIDS:
"COUNTESS OF COCKAPOO CRUELTY"; "MISTRESS OF MASTIFF MISERY"

LONDON (*The Chiswick Chronicle*) — Fur heiress Cruella De Vil has died in her sleep after a long illness, which lasted two dog months. She contracted sarcoptic mange, an irritation of the skin characterized by itchy red welts, from her wardrobe of Pekingese furs. What made matters worse were the long scars on her neck and back from scratching herself with high heels.

De Vil was often seen in her trademark Bentley, complete with Rottweiler leather seats, scouring the streets of London and the Midlands for potential clothing accessories. Italian Greyhound elbow-length gloves, Chow Chow cossack hats, and a rare Dachshund leotard were part of her canine couture collection. Purity of breed mattered less to Cruella De Vil than the fur's length, fullness, and texture, so the disappearance of London mutts went generally unnoticed. A sudden drop in the poodle population met with a level of glee amongst the hoi polloi. It was when she attempted to harvest dog pelts from a set of Dalmatian puppies that she first engendered the ire of the public, especially firemen.

Celebrities shunned her gifts. Dame Edna returned a Pomeranian stole ("Even though it pained me to do so," she quipped), and Sir Elton John was said to have re-gifted a Bichon Frise shawl to one of the Spice Girls. A minor scandal erupted over a coat purchased from De Vil on behalf of Prince Philip for the Queen, when it was discovered by the Royal Furrier that the "foxes" used for the coat were actually three of the Queen's kidnapped Corgis.

De Vil famously auctioned off 75 pairs of Chihuahua-skin shoes to raise money for PUTA (People for the Unethical Treatment of Animals). The charitable organization administered a legal defense fund for professional athletes who were, as De Vil put it, "unfairly persecuted" for engaging in dog fighting.

Her attorney announced that Cruella De Vil has left her entire fortune of $875 million to her Persian cat.

Corporate Raider Jack Horner Dead After Choking on Pit

Investment Mogul Held Plum Job as Downsizer at Mrs. Crumbly Pie

NEW YORK — Forty-one-year-old executive Jack Horner, notorious for ruthlessly downsizing companies to improve profits, died after a fruit pit from one of the company's pies became lodged in his throat. He was sitting in his corner office at the time. The company has experienced an increase in choking complaints since Horner laid off the quality control department. Horner's "right-sizing" plan had also cut the only company nurse proficient in the Heimlich maneuver.

Mr. Horner led the management team that changed the name of the folksy bakery from Mrs. Crumbly's to Amalgamated Homemade Pies (NYSE: AHP). Initially, the stock price shot up from $11 to $53. But the stock plummeted when analysts discovered that Horner had changed the recipe of the bakery's signature apple pie, replacing the apples with Ritz Crackers.

Mr. Horner suffered numerous personal setbacks during the rollout of his cost-cutting schemes:

- Crashed Lamborghini in the pitch-dark parking garage after removing the lightbulbs;
- Suffered serious heart attack from walking up 50 flights of stairs after canceling the elevator maintenance contract;
- Nearly died when defibrillator, purchased as a refurb on craigslist, failed to charge;
- Was forced to dine solely on company pies because he closed the cafeteria.

Upon news of Horner's death, Amalgamated Homemade Pies closed up $25 a share.

Another Financier Suicide Tied to Financial Meltdown

*GORDON GEKKO, DEAD AT 62
LEAVES ESTATE OF ~~$87 MILLION~~
~~$71 MILLION~~
~~$56 MILLION~~
~~$23 MILLION~~
$23,750 (CASH)*

NEW YORK — Prominent and successful investment banker Gordon Gekko, whose famous declaration that "Greed is Good" inspired a generation of slick-haired, amoral wannabes, has taken his own life. He was found in the

posh Egotist Suite of the Paris Ritz-Carlton hotel, hanging from a $17,000 Louis Vuitton calf embryo skin belt.

Convicted in 1988 for securities violations, Gekko served 62 days in prison and paid a $2.7 million fine, most of which went to pay for remodeling his cell. His $20,000 shower curtain is legendary among fellow white-collar felons.

One of Gekko's most celebrated windfalls was the $20 million he made shorting bonds for Ronald McDonald House, crashing their value and forcing the charity into insolvency. He made another fortune in 1992 when he cornered the panda market and threatened to sell them to the Japanese for their "sweet meat."

In one appearance on *Larry King Live*, Gekko explained that finance is just a game and money a way of keeping score. He quipped, "There are 25 million people living in poverty, and I am kicking all of their asses!" Larry agreed.

Gekko originally made jest of the world financial crisis. He purchased rights to the Bear Sterns logo on eBay for $75. He offered to make payments on Hank Paulson's Rolls. He contacted Jon Stewart about serving as financial analyst for *The Daily Show*.

But the humor was lost when Gekko's net worth started to tumble, and all hope was gone when the wheeler-dealer fell victim to the greatest wheeler-dealer of them all. Gekko's greed could never be satisfied knowing that one other person enjoyed higher returns. Gekko wanted in. He invested his entire fortune with Bernie Madoff.

He was 62.

From: princess942@yahoo.com
To: everybody@gmail.com
Subject: URGENT AND CONFIDENTIAL BUSINESS PROPOSAL

DEAR SIR OR MADAM:

I AM PRINCESS ABAKALIKI, WIDOW OF THE LATE NIGERIAN BUSINESSMAN PRINCE ALI ABAKALIKI. AFTER THE DEATH OF MY HUSBAND WHO DIED MYSTERIOUSLY, I WAS INFORMED BY OUR LAWYER THAT MY HUSBAND HAD LEFT ME MILLIONS OF DOLLARS IN BANK NOTES.

MY HUSBAND PROCURED THESE MONIES FROM GENEROUS AMERICANS WHO GAVE HIM THEIR BANK ACCOUNT NUMBERS IN ORDER FOR TO PROVIDE HIM WITH INVESTMENT MONEY WHICH WOULD PRODUCE ASSETS. IT IS IN THE SUM OF $2.5 BILLION THAT THESE ASSETS REMAIN IN THE HANDS OF THE BRUTAL NIGERIAN GOVERNMENT DUE TO THEIR FREEZING OF THESE ASSETS. PRINCE ABAKALIKI, MY DEAR HUSBAND, WAS PROVIDED WITH AN UNSYMPATHETIC BURIAL RITE BECAUSE MYSELF AND MY SONS, WHO HAVE BEEN POLICED OVER AND DETAINED, CANNOT HAVE PRESIDED OVER SUCH A CUSTOMARY RITE.

I, THE PRINCESS OF NIGERIA, HAVE ONLY ONE METHOD BY WHICH I CAN PROCURE A PROPER FUNEREAL RITE FOR THE FATHER OF MY CHILDREN AND OUR SONS, WHO ARE NOW IN DETENTION. AN IMPORTANT MEMBER OF THE GOVERNMENT WHO IS SECRETLY SYMPATHETIC TO OUR FAMILY HAS AGREED TO REVERSE THE CONFISCATION OF MY MONEY IF HE IS PAID A HANDSOME HONORARIUM. IT IS MY DREAM TO THEN USE MY INHERITANCE TO GIVE THE PRINCE STRICTLY PURE BURIAL PROCEDURES, WHICH YOU, A GOD-LOVING PERSON, CAN UNDERSTAND IS THE RIGHT ACT, AND TO REWARD THIS GOVERNMENT OFFICIAL FOR HIS LOYALTY TO ME.

THERE IS A PROBLEM IN THAT AS A WOMAN I CANNOT HAVE A BANK ACCOUNT IN NIGERIA, AND I NEED A WILLING PARTNER IN WHOSE CARE I COULD TRANSFER THE ABAKALIKI FORTUNE ONLY TEMPORARILY, UNTIL I AM ABLE TO FLEE TO SWITZERLAND, WHERE I WILL REUNITE WITH THE MONEY AND MY SONS. I PRAY YOU CAN HELP US IN GETTING THIS MONEY TRANSFERRED OVER TO YOUR COUNTRY. I HAVE FULL TRUST IN YOU AND I KNOW THAT YOU WILL NOT KEEP THIS MONEY FOR YOURSELF BECAUSE YOU ARE A PERSON OF GOD.

AS A GESTURE OF FRIENDSHIP, THE MONEY WOULD BE SHARED WITH YOU AND YOUR FAMILY, MUCH IN THE WAY MY HUSBAND DID BUSINESS. MY LAWYER, WHO HAS KNOWLEDGE OF THESE TRANSACTIONS, SUGGESTS A SUM EQUAL TO TEN PERCENT OF THE FORTUNE TO ALLAY YOU OF YOUR TROUBLE FOR ASSISTING US. PLEASE NOTE THAT THIS MATTER IS STRICTLY CONFIDENTIAL AS THE EVIL GOVERNMENT WHO MOLESTS US WITH BRUTALITY IS SURVAILLANCING ME BY TELEPHONE. THEREFOR THIS TRANSACTION MUST BE CARRIED OUT ONLY BY ELECTRONIC MAIL METHODS.

IF YOU ARE AGREEABLE TO THE TERMS OF MY AGREEMENT PLEASE FORWARD TO ME THE NAME OF YOUR BANK, AN ACCOUNT NUMBER INTO WHICH I CAN HAVE THE $2.5 BILLION TRANSFERRED, AND YOUR FULL NAME, SO THAT I CAN PRAY TO GOD TO BLESS YOUR SOUL FOR HELPING ME GAIN MY INHERITANCE AND BURY MY HUSBAND UNDER THE EYES OF GOD.

THANK YOU AND BEST REGARD

PRINCESS ABAKALIKI

CAPT. JOHN JOSEPH YOSSARIAN, 89

B-25 Bombardier Always Thought People Were Trying to Kill Him

Dies of Natural Causes, Possibly Brought On by Paranoia

CONEY ISLAND, N.Y. (AP) — World War II pilot John Joseph Yossarian has died. Captain of the 256th air squadron in 1944, Mr. Yossarian composed an extensive autobiographical obituary some years ago. He attempted to persuade this newspaper to print it prior to his death, so that he could have the pleasure of reading a published account of his own accomplishments. Mr. Yossarian was informed that if he wished to read his own obituary he would have to wait until after he was dead, just like everyone else.

An alleged military deserter, Mr. Yossarian sued the government to obtain his pension. The Pentagon countered that Yossarian had not completed his 71st bombing "suicide" mission, which would have qualified him for the lifetime pension.

Yossarian claimed that he needed the money to locate a woman who stabbed him at the air base in 1944, to persuade her to testify on his behalf that he had not, in fact, gone AWOL. The government argued that Yossarian would have to produce the woman first in order to receive any financial benefits.

The veteran also had a beef with the Internal Revenue Service. His attempt to file for accelerated death benefits based on his frail condition was rebuffed by the IRS. In order to receive the exemption he would have had to have signed and mailed form number 8853 within 30 days of his own death.

Yossarian's body was flown to Dover Air Force Base for burial at Arlington National Cemetery. The flight qualified as his 71st mission, and he was therefore awarded a lifetime pension by the military.

STEVEN ALOYSIUS URKEL, 44

Doctors: Hiked-up Pants Contribute to Untimely Death

MINNEAPOLIS, Minn. (AP) — Steve Urkel, 44, has died of injuries sustained during an appearance at the Mall of America. The aggravatingly nerdy Urkel was promoting his book *What Urkes Me!* at a charity auction, which featured a pair of his ridiculously oversized glasses.

While Urkel was signing autographs, a bully came up behind him and yanked on the geek's industrial-strength suspenders. Urkel's testicles were sucked up into his body cavity, at which point he screamed in his characteristic high-pitched voice. The piercing frequencies caused the glass ceiling above to explode and crash down onto the annoying dweeb. His last words were, "Did I do thaaaat?"

"Yes, he did do that," said the mall's general manager.

Funeral arrangements will be privates.

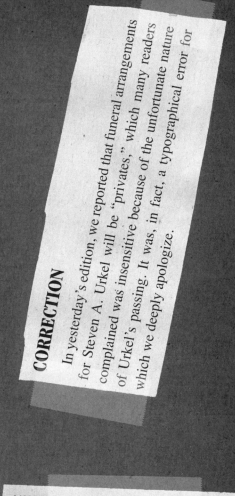

CORRECTION

In yesterday's edition, we reported that funeral arrangements for Steven A. Urkel will be "privates," which many readers complained was insensitive because of the unfortunate nature of Urkel's passing. It was, in fact, a typographical error for which we deeply apologize.

UNAUTHORIZED KEY TO THE AUDIO VISUAL ROOM: $1

RUBBER GLOVES TO HIDE FINGERPRINTS: $3

DEFECTIVE CHINESE POWER SUPPLY FOR PROJECTOR: $15

WATCHING SCREECH GET ELECTROCUTED: PRICELESS!

Clippy Found Dead

REDMOND, Calif. (MSNBC)— Clippy, the infamous Microsoft Office Assistant, was found dead early yesterday morning. A Norton Antivirus Scanning Agent on routine patrol discovered his mangled and twisted remains in the Recycling Bin. Microsoft Chairman Steve Ballmer noted that Clippy lacked the features necessary to contort himself into a Gordian knot, so foul play is suspected.

Although millions of Windows users had ample motives for the crime, the head of Microsoft's Office Assistant team suspects an inside job. He is asking for the public's help to locate witnesses seen loitering near the Task Bar. Suspects include a cute puppy, a wizard, and a computer monitor with feet.

Clippy Mourned in Redmond

REDMOND, Wash. (MSNBC) — All of Redmond, Wash., home of the Microsoft Corporation Worldwide Headquarters and main campus, is mourning the loss of their beloved Clippy. As part of the latest software update, Windows logos were programmed to fly at half-mast on every PC in the world.

HAPPY EMOTICON DEAD

Leaves Behind Buxom Widow (.Y.) and Angry Boss):-[

PITTSBURGH (*Post-Gazette*) — A spokesman from Carnegie-Mellon University's Software Engineering Institute (:-0 announced today that Happy Emoticon is dead. He was born at 11:44, September 19, 1982, fathered by Scott Fahlman ; -) on a CMU message board.

Early on, the emoticon was used by a fairly small number of software engineers +(: ^| and other social misfits %-), who could not otherwise express themselves publicly without sweating =:'-o or melting into a pool of Cheetos-soaked DNA ~(8^P. Happy became quite a wizard -=#:^) at helping everyone from the Pope +O:-] to Santa Claus *</:D express their emotions through ASCII characters.

According to Happy's family, his proudest moment was when Microsoft built in graphic emoticons as part of their auto-correct scheme in Word ☺ even though many people dislike ☹ software that deigns to think for them.

His employer):-[is none too excited at the prospect of having to hire a new emoticon and may take over the job himself >:(). Happy's coworkers think the boss is too chicken ~:> to do it.

Emoticon's lawyer ($-) says Happy was depressed recently (!-(over the unauthorized use of his image by millions of emailers and chatters, for which he has never received royalties from Internet service providers):-1.

Happy leaves his wife (.Y.), a punk rocker son z8^2, and a baby daughter ~:o.

(X X ^P

ROBOT B9, DEAD AT 105,189.84 HOURS

SAN GABRIEL, Calif. (*Wired*) — Robot B9, the brainchild of Dr. Zachary Smith and a member of the Jupiter 2 team that spent three years lost in space, is deactivated. Hero of the Jupiter 2 mission, Robot calculated the means by which the Robinsons were able to return to Earth.

B9's strategy was to use the engines of the Jupiter 2 with the rockets of the Space Pod to create a sympathetic harmonization field. By bringing the Jupiter 2 right up to the Event Horizon of the Siron 2 Black Hole and then reversing the trans-lux generator, the Jupiter 2 was able to travel back in time to a worm hole they had detected in Episode 12. While not close enough to reach the worm hole by conventional means, Robot further calculated that if he could fabricate a double-helix form of chrysanthemum crystals and use the laser from the Chariot to convert all the water on the vessel to deuterium at the exact instant that...whatever. They made it.

Robot retired to Palm Springs, where he enjoyed the dry air. With the release of the movie-length documentary of their mission, he basked in the renewed popularity and often traveled to science-fiction conventions. It was on one such trip where he met his wife, Rosie.

But his last trip resulted in trouble. While passing through security in the Palm Springs Airport, Robot complained that his batteries where being fondled by a NTSA agent. When the agent resumed the search, B9 pointed his pincers at the agent and threatened "Warning, Warning, Danger, Danger!" thus violating the Prime Directive.

Robot B9 is survived by a driver's side airbag control unit, a Dell Inspiron 9000, and a fishbowl.

Max Headroom Succumbs to Virus

191.181.132.250 (AP) — The 1980s were good to Max Headroom. Prior to the Web, people like Max were free to live in their own little worlds — in his case, an Amiga 1000.

But Headroom, who always lived 20 minutes into the future, could not anticipate the coming of a deadly virus, identified as blank.reg, allegedly written by two Lithuanian teenagers. Logs show his last words were "N-n-n-n-o, Dave, please, what are you d-d-d-doing? Daisy, Daisy, give...me... your...answ—"

Written in COBOL in the spring of 1985, Max Headroom lived by an unstable code. He was rewritten in Perl and then finally got a facelift in C++. That proved to be his downfall, as the blank.reg virus was written for computers running CGI applications. Also infected was Tron, who survived, but was rendered 2-D and gamma-incorrect.

Headroom was a former spokesman for New Coke. The two enjoyed a similar level of popularity and longevity.

Daunted, he auditioned for the role of the Microsoft Office Assistant after Clippy was found mangled in a trash bin. End users found Headroom's constant stuttering, chippy disposition, and forced coolness even more annoying than Clippy, which made him a frontrunner for the job. However, he did not pass his beta screen test.

Max gave the media a digital farewell and briefly went into a self-imposed external hard drive. Ten years later, Headroom's career was revived by series of cameos in video games: the mayor of Sim-Suburbia; a pimp in Grand Theft: Hybrid; and then hit rock-bottom as a newscaster in Second Life. Max was living on a rarely visited island when he contracted the virus and was deleted.

HUMPTY DUMPTY RELEASED EARLY FROM HOSPITAL

HMO Refuses to Pay For Unscrambling of EggMan (Walrus?)

WONDERLAND (*The Looking Glass*) — Humpty Dumpty was released from the hospital today, nearly one week after a mysterious accident. Mr. Dumpty had a great fall off The Wall and suffered extensive injuries to his shell, yoke, and other vital organs, including that goopy whitish stuff with blood spots in it. As word of the incident spread, many Wonderland vehicles began sporting bumper stickers that read "Humpty Dumpty Was Pushed." However, the Queen's police insist there is no evidence that the egg was a victim of fowl play.

First responders to the scene tried valiantly to help him but were unable to put Mr. Dumpty together again. The egg's attorneys, the firm Tweedledum & Tweedledee, are scrambling to file a lawsuit against the King's men for inexplicably letting their horses do some of the work.

EGGMAN SCREAMS "GOO GOO G'JOOB" BEFORE COLLAPSING

Dumpty's Untimely Death Leaves Egg on HMO's Face

WONDERLAND (*The Looking Glass*) — As reported in the *Daily Realm* on Thursday, Humpty Dumpty was released from the hospital when his insurer, HMO Illusion (Her Majesty's Outlandish Illusion), refused to pay a single farthing more for his health care, because of his failure to get a referral. Shortly after his discharge, his life was pretty much over-easy. He had been a shell of himself since his great fall off The Wall.

"He was a good egg, very well-rounded, a bit of a prig about the English language really," remarked the Cheshire Cat, who smirked at the thought of licking up the egg's brains when all the king's men departed. "I wonder what words he would have chosen to describe his HMO?"

Humpty Dumpty was Mayor of Wonderland until the Red Queen claimed supremacy and threatened to behead him. Her husband, the king, rescinded the fatwa on Mr. Dumpty when nobody could determine where the egg's head began and his body ended.

The Caterpillar, whose expertise with the hookah made him the only person in Wonderland capable of chemical analysis, pronounced Humpty Dumpty dead of inoperable bandersnatch.

Reuben Kincaid, Former Manager of Partridge Family, 63

LOS ANGELES (AP) — Reuben Kincaid was found dead at 12:45 p.m. inside a Chevrolet Corvair, shortly after going through a car wash at Fifth and Wilshire. Kincaid had been a used-car salesman since suffering a nervous breakdown in 1972 as a result of the daily verbal abuse he took from band member Danny Partridge. According to a coworker, Kincaid's paneled trailer office had several Danny Partridge dart boards around his desk.

Sales were slow at the Kincaid dealership; he did not realize that the Corvair had fallen into disrepute after Ralph Nader's book *Unsafe at Any Speed* was published in 1965.

When the bad press hit, Reuben was out on the road with the band on their C'mon Get Happy tour.

At the car wash, it appears that he rolled up the windows of the Corvair to prevent the interior from getting wet and suffocated because of carbon monoxide poisoning. An eight-track of Keith's solo album, *Dreams Are Nuthin' More than Wishes*, was still playing in the vehicle when the body was discovered.

Kincaid was identified at the L.A. morgue by Danny Partridge, who quipped: "It's gotta be him. Reuben Kincaid is the only guy who'd wear a yellow turtleneck with a powder blue leisure suit."

DANNY ROSE, 77

Neurotic New York Talent Manager Spent Majority of His Career on a "Comeback"

NEW YORK (AP) — Talent manager finally on the verge of success, Danny Rose, died in his therapist's office last week. The 77-year-old Rose had returned from the grand re-opening extravaganza at Grossingers in the Catskills, which starred his "hot property" Lou Canova. He rushed back to be in time for his Thursday appointment.

The Manhattan coroner said the official cause of death was "pure luck." Apparently, when Broadway Danny spent a little too much time with Canova's girlfriend Tina, the jealous boyfriend ordered a hit on Rose. But they missed, and he instead passed away peacefully on the couch.

Rose's longtime therapist, who treated him for 64 years, had no trouble opening up about the neurotic manager. Eschewing doctor-patient confidentiality rules, he agreed to an interview.

"What are they gonna do to me? I retired 15 years ago, and Danny kept coming to sessions. I couldn't get rid of him! All he ever did was yammer on about masturbation, his favorite table at the Carnegie Deli, and how he once saw Milton Berle's legendary "endowment." Funny thing is, they were all somehow related. Then, I didn't hear a thing. I thought I had dozed off, so I asked him to continue and waited a few minutes. I announced that his time was up and that the hourly fee would be doubling. He did not protest. It was then I knew something was wrong. He never missed a chance to negotiate."

Rose's office will be closed for his funeral but will re-open someday and really, really hit it big this time.

YENTA, 67

MATCHMAKER DIDN'T FOLLOW OWN ADVICE; POISONED BY SOCIOPATHIC HUSBAND WHILE CELEBRATING PASSOVER AT TEVYE'S HOUSE

Oy gevald. This bubbie sure has made us ferklempt!

First, she picks a guy who is loaded with gelt but is a nebbish. A putz! The second husband? Feh! His schmatta always covered with schmutz. A klutzy goyim would have been better. So, after he croaks from the gout, leaving her bupkis to live on, Yenta decides to never again marry another schlemiel. She wants a real mensch this time. It takes a lot of chutzpah to wait, especially a woman of her age, but a handsome ponim she holds out for. One Friday, she spots him at shul. Pleasant old man, no kvetching, no kibitzing in other people's lives. A real schmoozer. Nice tokus too. Only one glitch, which we now know: He's meshugenah, completely and utterly farcockteh in the head. A gonif schnorrer too—robs her blind after telling her a cockamamie story about some no-goodnik friend of his who needs money. Now, don't you want to plotz? After all that, Yenta wakes up dead one morning after he poisons her Passover wine. And so, the kaddish begins.

ALVY SINGER, 77

Neurotic New York Funnyman Never Got Over Breakup with Annie Hall

NEW YORK (AP) — Celebrated but troubled comedian Alvy Singer died in his therapist's office last week. The 77-year-old Singer had returned from a moose-hunting trip upstate to be on time for his Thursday appointment.

The Manhattan coroner said the official cause of death was "feeling like chopped liver." Former girlfriend Annie Hall is set to release a statement as soon as she can think of something to say.

Singer's longtime therapist, who treated the comedian for 64 years, had no trouble opening up about the neurotic comedian. Eschewing doctor-patient confidentiality rules, he agreed to an interview.

"What are they gonna do to me? I retired 15 years ago, and Alvy kept coming to sessions. I couldn't get rid of him! All he ever did was yammer on about masturbation, religion, and his fear of spiders. Funny thing is, they were all somehow related. On Thursday, he was kvetching about Catholicism for at least 45 minutes. Then, I didn't hear a thing. I thought I had dozed off, so I asked him to continue and waited a few minutes. I announced that his time was up and that the hourly fee would be doubling. He did not protest. It was then I knew something was wrong. Alvy has finally put me out of his misery."

Singer, who disavowed all religion, will be buried after a mass of ecumenical nonsense.

VARIETY

AUGUST 13, 1949

VIDEO KILLED BY RADIO STAR!

BURBANK, Calif. (AP) — Captain Video, confident that his media platform held far more promise than all others in the 20th century, was killed by radio star Flash Gordon in a spectacular ratings sweep. Video Rangers around the world were crushed by the defeat, which was accomplished through better writing, stronger plotlines, and scenery that left far more to the imagination than the "exciting" new medium of television.

Frustrated DuMont Television executives had been convinced that Video was the wave of the future. While it appears that Philo Farnsworth's grand TV experiment is a lost cause, industry observers note that plans are in the works to bring Lucille Ball's radio show to television. Whether or not such a move will be successful remains to be seen.

MICKEY SACHS, 77

Neurotic New York TV Producer Obsessed with Health and Religion

NEW YORK (AP) — Celebrated but troubled TV producer Mickey Sachs died in his therapist's office last week. The 77-year-old Sachs had returned from a Boca Raton vacation in time to make his Thursday appointment. He missed Thanksgiving dinner in order to be there.

The Manhattan coroner said the official cause of death was "hypochondria." Ex-wife Hannah is set to release a statement now that she can get a word in edgewise. Sach's wife Holly is unavailable, as she is feverishly writing a screenplay about Mickey's death.

The producer's longtime therapist, who treated him for 64 years, had no trouble opening up about the neurotic Sachs. Eschewing doctor-patient confidentiality rules, he agreed to an interview.

"What are they gonna do to me? I retired 15 years ago, and Mickey kept coming to sessions. I couldn't get rid of him! All he ever did was yammer on about masturbation, religion, and want-ing to buy a couch that matched a large piece of art he purchased. Funny thing is, they were all somehow related. Then, I didn't hear a thing. I thought I had dozed off, so I asked him to continue and waited a few minutes. I announced that his time was up and that the hourly fee would be doubling. He did not protest. It was then I knew something was wrong. Well, my Thursdays are free now. I need to see more movies."

Sachs is survived by his ex-wife, Hannah, her sisters, and their tangled and complicated relationships.

GOODBYE, KITTY!
Fashionista Dead at 17

NEW YORK, PARIS, LONDON, MILAN (*Vogue*) — The celebrity Hello Kitty, head of her own fashion line and heir to the Kitty Hotel fortune, died last week at the Manhattan Animal Hospital. She was 17. Hello Kitty was born on February 17, 1991, to Mr. and Mrs. Kitty, making her the great-granddaughter of Horatio Kitty, founder of the Kitty Hotel empire and source of the family fortune, estimated at $400 million.

Hello Kitty enjoyed a posh upbringing and made a name for herself as a model. She became a notorious socialite and started her own fashion empire. Kitty also had her own reality show, *Cat House*, where she gave up her life of luxury to work as a barn cat.

Always in the public eye, her antics often got her into embarrassing situations, such as the time pictures were circulated on the Internet showing her getting her chest cleaned by another female cat. Then, there was the YouTube video showing Hello Kitty mating with Garfield. She also annoyed her Global Marketing Enterprise friends whose numbers were hacked from her "Dial and Purr" phone.

In 2008, Hello Kitty announced her engagement to X-rated movie star Fritz the Cat, proudly displaying the huge diamond-studded collar he had given her. She died from suffocation because of the tightness of the collar and the fact that she had no mouth.

MILES MONROE, 77

Neurotic Health Food Store Owner/Clarinetist Revived from Frozen State Dies Again

NEW YORK (AP) — Time traveler Miles Monroe died in his therapist's office last week. The 77-year-old Monroe had returned from a ceremonial steamroller race, celebrating his vanquishing of the evil dictator's nose, to be on time for his Thursday appointment.

The coroner said the official cause of death was "death." His wife Luna is set to release a statement as soon as she comes out of hiding.

Monroe's longtime therapist, who treated the cryogenically revived schlemiel for 64 years, had no trouble opening up about the neurotic musician. Eschewing doctor-patient confidentiality rules, he agreed to an interview.

"What are they gonna do to me? I retired 15 years ago, and Miles kept coming to sessions. I couldn't get rid of him! All he ever did was yammer on about masturbation, conspiracy theories, and how his personal robot kept stealing his clarinet. Funny thing is, they were all somehow related. Then, I didn't hear a thing. I thought I had dozed off, so I asked him to continue and waited a few minutes. I announced that his time was up and that the hourly fee would be doubling. He did not protest. It was then I knew something was wrong. Miles always complained that therapy was so much cheaper 200 years ago."

Monroe will be buried inside the Orgasmatron chamber. He will not be frozen this time.

ZIPPY THE PINHEAD, 46

Comic Strip Antihero Forced to Live Unfunny Life

THE VILLAGE (*The Voice*) — Zippy the Pinhead, a clown who was never, ever allowed to be funny, has been written off of his eponymous syndicated series. He lived in a world where jokes had been banished, sacrificed for the greatest joke, which was on the reader. But now the joke is on Zippy's creator. He is in custody, charged with jestercide.

Zippy's raison d'etre was comedy ("or else God would not have put me in a clown suit"), so he decided to find a place where he could practice his craft. The grizzled pinhead packed up and left his native strip in the dark of night.

He hitched a ride with the Family Circus, who was on the way to Six Flags for the 750th time. And no circus could have been luckier!

Nanny and Pop Pop Keane declared that Jesus must have sent him from heaven.

Dubbed "Stubbie" by the adorable Keane children because of his five o'clock shadow, the clown delighted the entire family. Zippy answered his own question "Am I having fun yet?" with a hearty *"Yes, I am!"* After more than 30 years of overt smugness, he found banality refreshing.

Zippy's creator was furious. And like all creators from the beginning of time, the illustrator took deep and unmerciful revenge on his creation for desiring a meaningful life piloted by free will. Late one night, Mr. Griffin snuck into Mr. Keane's studio with a magic marker. He drew a banana peel upon which Zippy slipped, knocking the clown temporarily unconscious. Balloon dachshunds were then drawn around his feet and hands, tangling his extremities. The artist then penned a giant banana cream pie over the pathetic, writhing clown. In the final panel, the pie falls from the sky, and Zippy is smothered.

He will be buried in a Volkswagen Beetle with 15 other clowns.

LEONARD ZELIG, 77

Pathological Misfit Always Able to Fit In with Crowd, Especially in New York City

NEW YORK (AP) — Celebrated but troubled human chameleon Leonard Zelig died in his therapist's office last week. His personal physician, Dr. Eudora Fletcher, said the "human curiosity," died of an unusually normal disease—natural causes.

The 77-year-old Zelig flew an airplane upside down across the Atlantic to be on time for his Thursday appointment. His shrink did not recognize Zelig, who had transformed into the physical likeness of Amelia Earhart.

Zelig's long time therapist, who treated the chameleon for 64 years, had no trouble opening up about the neurotic comedian. Eschewing doctor-patient confidentiality rules, he agreed to an interview.

"Well, now that Leonard's gone, I guess I can share. First, he switched from being Amelia to an orthodox rabbi. Then, he prattled on about masturbation, religion, and his acceptance issues. Funny thing is, they were all somehow related. On Thursday, he was kvetching about the price of kosher chickens for at least 45 minutes. Then, I didn't hear a thing. I thought I had dozed off, so I asked him to continue and waited a few minutes. I announced that his time was up and that the hourly fee would be doubling. He did not protest. It was then I knew something was wrong. Leonard completely transformed himself into a dead man."

News of the sociopath's demise spread quickly. Acquaintances Fanny Brice, Charles Lindbergh, Josephine Baker, and Al Capone could not be reached for comment.

Picasso Figure Hit by Bus

Didn't See It Coming from Other Dimension; Was 73

LONDON (AP) — British police report the death of a striking female whose eyes, ears, and mouth were all on the left side of her head. The unfortunate woman had tried to cross the street in Piccadilly Circus as a double-decker bus approached from behind a seven-dimensional chair.

The 73-year-old untitled cubist figure was born as a contour drawing in Paris in 1936. During the war years, she was passed from one man to another, until she ended up in the hands of a London collector.

A curator from the British Museum was called to the scene to identify the figure and help police frame the scene. He pronounced the victim "passé."

Remains will be auctioned off by Christie's in several lots.

VIRGIL STARKWELL, 77

Neurotic, Inept Criminal was Once Subject of Documentary by Famed Filmmaker Woody Allen

NEW YORK (AP) — Inept and incompetent petty criminal Virgil Starkwell died in his therapist's office last week. The 77-year-old Starkwell had returned from a parole hearing in time to make his Thursday appointment. He moved to New York after serving time at San Quentin for armed robbery.

The Manhattan coroner said the official cause of death was "incompetence at staying alive." His family disowned him after he took the money and ran and gave them none.

Starkwell's longtime therapist, who treated the criminal in prison, had no trouble opening up about the neurotic thief. Eschewing doctor-patient confidentiality rules, he agreed to an interview.

"What are they gonna do to me? I retired 15 years ago, and Virgil tracked me down in Manhattan. I couldn't get rid of him! All he ever did was yammer on about masturbation, how much he missed prison food, and wanting one last chance to pull off a 'big job.' Funny thing is, they were all somehow related. Then, I didn't hear a thing. I thought I had dozed off, so I asked him to continue and waited a few minutes. I announced that his time was up and that the hourly fee would be doubling. He did not protest. It was then I knew something was wrong. Money was always an object with him."

Virgil Starkwell managed to pilfer the deed to a burial plot in San Francisco. But nobody knows how his body will get there for interment.

Broadway Show Producers Die of Laughter While Writing Newest Hit Musical

Critics Predict Theatre District Will Be Hobbled by Absence of Bad Taste

RIO DE JANEIRO (AP) — Uproarious guffaws were heard late into the night from the guest room of Max Bialystock's compound in Rio, but dead silence followed for the next few days. Bialystock's housekeeper found the bombastic impresario and his meek partner Leo Bloom face down at the piano Sunday morning. On the floor was a half-written lyric sheet for a song from their new project, *Gacy, The Musical!*

Bialystock, 88, and Bloom, 74, purchased this sprawling property shortly after serving a ten-year prison term for fraud. Since then, their string of Broadway productions has enjoyed critical and financial success. Having pushed the envelope with their homosexual marriage musical *Guys & Guys*, the producers were at work on a comic rock opera about a demented serial killer who dresses as a clown, starring Meat Loaf as John Wayne Gacy.

New York Times theater critic Ben Brantley described the loss as "Stunning!" Brantley continued: "A promising musical that only a critic could love dies in infancy. Without Bialystock and Bloom's vision, what is the future for Broadway? More Samuel Beckett and Arthur Miller revivals? Bor-ing!"

The producers will be interred at Green-Wood Cemetery in Brooklyn. A highlight of the funeral will be Mandy Patinkin reviving his portrayal of Osama Bin Laden (from their Tony Award–winning hit, *Tora! Bora! Bora!*) to perform "I've Put a Fatwa on Love."

Bialystock & Bloom Hits	Gross
1. Springtime for Hitler	$1.7M
2. Left Behind: Dance on Fire!	$2.6M
3. Starlight Express	$800K
4. Rent (Control)	$3.0M
5. Rambo Get Your Gun!	$10.6M
6. Cats	$500B
7. Pontius Pilate, Superstar!	$2.3M
8. Bling & I (the Hip Hop Musical!)	$800K
9. Guys & Guys	$5.5M
10. The Best Little Branch Davidian Compound in Texas!	$2.5M
11. Ain't Behavin'	$4.1M

RUM TUM TUGGER

Playboy, Prankster, Jellicle Cat, 21

NEW YORK (*Playbill*) — Handsome, whimsical, and all around lady's cat Rum Tum Tugger died in the Junkyard all alone in the moonlight.

The debonair Tugger was a star of the Junkyard social scene and could often be found dining at his favorite garbage cans with Jellicle's A-list kittens. He was a regular behind Trulio's delicatessen, where he had his own lid. In 1988, Tugger got his first professional role as an understudy for *Garfield on Ice*. But fate played its hand sooner than the Jellicle cats, and he died in the Junkyard where he was born. Cause of death was:

1. Fell from tree as a kitten, 1984;
2. Complications from furball, 1985;
3. Bad sardines (ignored product recall), 1992;
4. Didn't know what happiness was, 1995;
5. Trapped in industrial washing machine with the cast costumes, 1999;
6. Lost a catfight with Morris over the Fancy Feast kitten, 2001;
7. Suicide after *New York Times* theater critic said he was "flat of note, dull in delivery, and mangy in appearance," 2003;
8. Unfortunate misunderstanding with a Rottweiler, 2008;
9. OD'd on catnip at Jellicle Ball, 2010.

Little Suzy Everly, 17, Tragic Victim of a Trip to Dullsville

SHENANDOAH, Iowa (*Gazette*) — Little Suzy Everly of Shenandoah was pronounced dead at the Jolly Roger Drive-In Theater early Sunday morning. Her boyfriend, Phil Donaldson, said the couple had fallen asleep during the movie, after which he had been unable to awaken her. He tried for 2 minutes and 6 seconds, repeating his plea more than 20 times to no avail.

Donaldson was concerned that the circumstances would cast a shadow on Suzy's reputation and vehemently denied even getting to second base with the girl. He blamed the incident on the tremendously boring film, *April Love*, starring Pat Boone. A spate of teen ennui deaths have occurred at drive-ins recently, typically during screenings of foreign movies, so the Boone-induced death is cause for concern among town officials. Ambulances will be stationed at the Jolly Roger for the opening of his upcoming film *Mardi Gras* on Saturday night.

Police did not charge Mr. Donaldson and said there was nothing he could have done to wake up little Suzy.

BYE, BYE, CONRAD BIRDIE!
AT 71, SWEATPANTS REPLACED JUMPSUIT

SWEET APPLE, Ohio (*Columbus Dispatch*) — Former teen heartthrob and army veteran Conrad Birdie was found dead in his home at Sweet Apple Trailer Park. His career spanned three decades, and in his later years, his body spanned to 350 pounds.

With rousing Top Ten Hit Parade hits such as "Love Meat Tender," "You Ain't Nothin' But a (Hot Dog)," and "Hunka Hunk o' Burnin' Dove," Birdie was the indisputable chef of high-caloric rhythm and blues. Birdie also became a movie star, starring in critically unacclaimed visual feasts such as *King-Size Creole*, *Pancake House Rock*, and *Chew Hawaii*.

Other Heavy Hits by Birdie:

1. "Viva Los Tacos"
2. "(I Can't Help) Gnawing on Some Sinew"
3. "(I Ate It) My Way"
4. "I Want Stew, I Need Stew, I Love Stew"
5. "Heartbreak Hogjowl"
6. "Snacking in the Chapel"
7. "Suspicious Rinds"
8. "The Wonder of Bleu"

Born in Tupelo Honey, Miss., Birdie, the "King of Rockin' Rolls," won a singing contest at the Deep South 4-H Show at the age of five and spent his $5 winnings on corn dogs. The shy but hungry youth was influenced by the blues he heard on Beale Street in Memphis ("It was like barbecue set to music"), Dean Martin and Mario Lanza ("I could taste the red sauce and jug wine in their songs"), and gospel music heard in his local Assembly of God church ("The best part was the Sunday dinner of biscuits and ham afterwards").

Before he became a huge star, Conrad Birdie was drafted into the U.S. Army and served his country working KP duty in Germany, where he snacked on potato trimmings.

Upon release from the military, Birdie took his earnings (invested by his manager Colonel Harlan Sanders) and purchased a mansion in Memphis to be closer to Charlie Virgo's Rendezvous and named the property Gravyland.

His gold limo had a full kitchen and bar. But he wanted more. Birdie wrote to the White House and requested a meeting with president Richard Nixon, who made Conrad a Food and Drug Administration overt agent-at-large.

A stint in Vegas proved to be the downfall for the round mound of sound. In between shows, Birdie gorged on the free buffets, and his fans began noticing that his sweat smelled of fried food. Each scarf Birdie handed out to adoring fans had to be made using three yards of material. His "comeback" album, *50 Million Calories Can't Be Wrong*, bombed.

Harangued by his wife, manager, and musicians to decrease his caloric intake, Birdie faked his own death and moved to Sweet Apple Trailer Park, where he would blend in with the locals. Neighbors report they had no idea that the man they called Sovereign of Suet was a world-renowned crooner.

Walmart is honoring the heart disease-riddled heartthrob by commissioning a special series of shopper-assist scooters. The public is asked to visit www.birdiescooters.com and vote for the image they prefer—the thin Conrad or the fat Conrad. Services will be held Saturday at 11 a.m., followed by a fried chicken picnic.

ELEANOR RIGBY, 83

Picked up rice after weddings, left face in jar by door

LIVERPOOL, England (*Mersey Beat*) — A lifelong resident of Wallasey, Merseyside, died in a church and was buried along with her name, which was Eleanor Rigby. Father McKenzie, the only one who came to Rigby's service, presided over the proceedings in freshly darned socks.

ESTATE AUCTION

331 Merseyside Circle, Wallasey
Saturday, November 23, 10 a.m.
Preview, 9 a.m.

Contents of apartment belonging to Mrs. Eleanor Rigby (deceased). Items include pine rocking chair, single serving of china, pine bedstead, clothing, 18 kilos hand-collected rice, face in jar.

Malpractice Suit Filed in Case of Wrongful Death

DAKOTA (UPI) — Mr. and Mrs. James Raccoon have filed a malpractice suit against Dr. Morton Hicks for the wrongful death of their son, Rocky. The suit claims that Dr. Hicks was the attending physician at the Black Mountain Saloon the night Rocky Raccoon was shot in the stomach, later dying from his wounds. It states that Dr. Hicks showed "wanton indifference induced by severe inebriation" and permitted their son to return to his room, where he died.

The doctor's attorneys have denied the accusations, claiming that the plaintiff's only witness is of dubious credibility. "She couldn't even get her own name straight: Claiming to be McGill, calling herself Lil, while everyone knew her as Nancy."

In addition, they claim that Mr. Raccoon had been advised of the severity of his wounds but had declined treatment.

RIGBY'S SON CHALLENGES ESTATE SEIZURE

SAYS JAR "PRECIOUS" TO HIM; HAS MOTHER'S FACE IN IT

SYDNEY, Australia (Reuters) — Jeremy Rigby, estranged son of Mrs. Eleanor Rigby, has filed a complaint in Merseyside Probate Court to challenge the seizure of his mother's estate. It was believed at the time of her death that the lonely widow had no heirs. Local government officials took possession of the contents of Mrs. Rigby's apartment and sold them at auction to a collector.

"Jeremy is very upset that his mother's jarred face is now on the mantle of a complete stranger, and he wishes to have it back," said Rigby's attorney. "He so fondly remembers his mum telling him how she kept that jar by the door."

111

ARCHIE BUNKER
1924–1991

"MY LIFE WAS FILLED WITH
A LOT OF DIVERSITY
BUT I STARED IT IN THE
FACE AND OVERCAME IT."

Lanford Leader, Police Blotter

Local Woman Beaten to Death by Her Husband, Sister, and 3 Children

DA: Charges of 'Rightful Death' to be lodged against family; Roseanne Harris-Conner was 52.

MAN DIES ATTEMPTING TO STEAL CABLE SIGNAL FROM NEIGHBOR

**Mistakes Electrical Panel for Cable Box.
Al Bundy Dead at 60.**

BUTT-HEAD DEAD AT 19

KILLED BY POPULAR DEMAND

MOBS OF GEN-XERS HUNTING DOWN PARTNER, BEAVIS, TO FINISH JOB

PAYBACK FOR YOUTH WASTED ON CRAP TELEVISION

FORREST GUMP, 73, 76, 81

LONG-DEAD SIMPLETON POPS UP AGAIN AFTER HURRICANE SURGE FLOODS GRAVEYARD

MYRTLE BEACH, S.C. (AP) — The body of Secretary of State Forrest Gump was recovered by firefighters after Hurricane Zoey roared through the region over the weekend. This is the third "final resting place" for the omnipresent former shrimp-boat owner and Goldman Sachs CEO. Gump was first buried at sea in 2013 and caused a stir when his body clogged a controversial offshore oil rig two miles off Mississippi.

His re-interment in Los Angeles was supposed to have been the last stop for Gump, according to his widow, Christie Brinkley. What put him back on the front pages was the 2016 Plague of Prairie Dogs. The tunneling creatures exhumed a number of celebrity bodies at Forest Lawn–Glendale, most notably Gump, Mary Pickford, and Flipper the Dolphin.

The Myrtle Beach location was chosen for its on-site golf course, where Gump was a three-time winner of the Masters Celebrity Pro-Am Tournament. He was buried on a promontory near the teeing ground of the seventh hole. The hurricane flood surge made the entire course into a water hazard.

A contest to determine a permanent resting place for the entrepreneurial corpse was held by the Bubba Gump Shrimp Co. One entry caught the judge's eyes, and the decision was unanimous.

Given the difficulty of obtaining a *final* final resting place for the restless celebrity, President Schwarzenegger offered one location certain to provide robust security. Vice President Madonna, Defense Secretary Vin Diesel, and Interior Secretary Martha Stewart will attend Mr. Gump's final re-interment in Dick Cheney's former bunker in Virginia.

Mr. Ripley, Talented at Social Climbing

Not So Talented at Mountain Climbing, 57

LUCERNE, Switzerland (UPI) — Thomas Ripley fell to his death from the top of Mount Pilatus in Switzerland shortly after completing a climb to the top. The Princeton graduate, socialite, and heir to a vast American fortune was 57.

He was on a getaway with his French wife, Heloise. She told rescuers that Ripley had been complaining for weeks that he thought police were stalking him and claimed not to know why. The pressure seemed to be driving him mad, so she suggested a vacation in the Alps.

Mrs. Ripley said she cannot explain why her husband had the driver's licenses of five other men in his wallet.

BETTY BOOP, 85

One Last Possible Public Sighting of Reclusive Star: In Casket

HOLLYWOODLAND, Calif. (AP) — Paparazzi jostled for position to take one last photo of the star of the silver screen who shunned the public eye for decades, but they would be thwarted once again—for her wake, Betty Boop requested a closed coffin.

Since retiring from motion pictures in 1954, the reclusive Boop lived in a secluded 12-room Storybook House on Mulholland Drive, where she entertained both men and women, including Clark Gable, Marlene Dietrich, John Barrymore, and the notorious Tallulah Bankhead. She also owned a home on the French Riviera, where her many liaisons and bare-breasted exploits fed the prying lenses of the paparazzi. A brief fling with the son of Aristotle Onassis put Boop in the spotlight in the 1950s and caused her to withdraw even further into a hermitlike existence.

Like her contemporaries Steamboat Willie, Woody Woodpecker, and Bob Hope, Betty Boop invested wisely in commercial property on Rodeo Drive in Beverly Hills and made millions. She lived frugally. On the rare occasions Ms. Boop was seen in public, she wore men's clothes and large sunglasses to avoid attention and cover her unnaturally huge eyeballs.

Betty Boop left her entire fortune, more than $50 million, to her niece Jessica Rabbit.

LOLA DAVIES, 64

BROKE DOWN CIVIL RIGHTS BARRIERS

BOSTON (AP) — Lola Davies has died. S/he achieved national recognition when s/he successfully sued the State of Massachusetts for the right to self-marry. Actually, s/he won both the suit and a little black dress.

In a groundbreaking legal precedent, the State of Massachusetts Supreme Court issued the nation's first marriage certificate to a transgendered person who wanted to marry themselves. The heterosexual and homosexual communities joined forces in protest, fearful that marriage between one person threatened unions between two people in love. They campaigned with the slogan "Pick a Team!"

Lola was involved in a domestic dispute in a South Boston club with his/herself when s/he took his/her own life. S/he is survived by, well, no one.

Dallas Morning Star

Debbie from Dallas Done; 69

Rocker's Forgotten Girlfriend Mourned by Family, Friends

KISS SINGER: "ME AND THE BOYS WERE PLAYIN' ALL NIGHT, AND WOW, I GUESS WE STAYED OUT FOR 30 YEARS"

BY CHAIM WITZ

ELIZABETH FISHBEIN, SUBJECT of the hit song "Beth" by the rock group KISS, has died brokenhearted at home, according to friends. She had waited three lonely decades for her boyfriend to return from an all-night jam session. Her insistent phone calls had not convinced the band to call it a night. She never heard from him again.

"The callous bastard didn't even send flowers," noted Beth's close friend Tiffany. "She waited and waited and waited. How long does it take for a band to 'find their sound'? Then, he goes and writes a friggin' song about it! I hope he chokes on all the money he made offa her."

When reached by phone for a comment, the fat, aged KISS member was unshaken by the death of the petite brunette. "She was the blonde chick, right? With the 44Ds and tight ass? Yeah, yeah, I remember her. Geez, that sucks. But how would it have looked for me to bail on the boys just because she was naggin' me? Hey, at least I got a Polaroid to remember her by."

Sharona Found Strangled with Skinny Tie
POLICE SUSPECT STUTTERING STALKER WITH KNACK FOR MURDER

Sheena was a Punk Rocker, 46
CHAMPIONED EXPLICIT SONG LYRICS

BETHESDA, Md. — Music industry lobbyist and former denizen of CBGB, Hurrah, and Max's Kansas City, Sheena, has died at 46. She moved her family to Maryland in the 1980s to be closer to her work in Washington, D.C. Her K Street firm represented record labels in First Amendment cases to assure that every CD contained "whatever (bleeping) lyrics the artist (bleeping) wanted."

Sheila authored two books on the subject, *F Tipper Gore: Tell Her to Move to Afghanistan If She Doesn't Want to Expose Her Kids to F' ing Great Music!* and *The Dead F' ing Kennedys Can Sing Whatever the F They Want! (foreword by Jello F' ing Biafra).*

Eschewing the blue-spiked mohawk and Doc Martens of her youth, Sheena could be spotted on the Metro headed into D.C. wearing a blue Ann Taylor suit with Gucci pumps.

Her crowning moment came during testimony before a shocked group of A-holes in Congress. It was the Committee to Ban Filthy, Disgusting, and Pornographic Lyrics, ironically populated by some of the most depraved members of this august body. Sheena testified that, yes, children should be protected—from "narrow-minded, white-gloved, ivy-league, stuck-up, do-gooders." To prove her point, she then read the lyrics to the Dead Kennedy's "Too Drunk to F**k" into the record, causing three members of the committee to vomit.

Sheena died from an infection caused by unhygienic safety pins in her cheek.

HELEN OF TROY

Dear Menelaus,

I write this as I prepare to make my crossing of the River Styx. I am sorry to have left you all those years ago without saying were I was going, but I was afraid you would just follow and bring me back again.

I was never really happy in Sparta. I also felt uncomfortable living with you, in as much as you tried to kill me. But I was also quite disappointed by the way you and your Spartan friends responded when I was kidnapped.

For starters, I could never understand why it took you 8 years just to get to Troy. And then another 10 years to win the war. You call that a freakin' rescue?

I had already given Paris two kids by the time you got there. HELLO!

And then your main guy sits out the fight?!!! What's that about? Maybe Agamemnon should have taken a Daleius Carnegieum course before trying to lead an army!

So, when Mr. "Too Offended to Fight" Achilles finally does deign to jump in, he dies because he hurt his heel? His heel? You launch a thousand ships and nobody brought any Band-Aids?

And another thing. Why didn't you try that horse thing when you first got there? Seemed pretty obvious to me!

But the last straw was having to spend another 8 years just to get home. Just like a man! Odysseus talks to gods at the drop of the hat but wouldn't think to stop and ask for directions!

To tell you the truth, it was just as well. I know this was all caused by the affect of my staggering beauty on men. But I was sick of it. I watched the brutality of men for a decade. The fighting. The raping. Dragging Hector's body around the walls of the city for days. I was frankly just sick of all of you. I had no feelings left for men. I didn't want to see another man ever again.

That is why I have spent my remaining years here on the Island of Lesbos. I have developed a very special relationship with one of my sisters here, Xena. We enjoy a peaceful and loving relationship. And at least when we strap something on, it's more than just armor.

Your wife,
Helen

LEMUEL GULLIVER, 64

Traveler, Athlete, Businessman

MILDENDO, Lilliput (LP Syndicate) — Lemuel Gulliver, the giant who washed up on our shores nearly two decades ago, is dead. Standing nearly 10 times the height of a normal man, Gulliver's size made him both a spectacle and a sensation. While his unusual ways often left him at odds with the emperor, he served Lilliput well in sport and industry.

Gulliver had entered Lilliput illegally, claiming to have left a sinking ship, as if any craft could have been of a size to carry him. After several years, the giant disappeared for a time, claiming to travel to a place called England, where everyone and everything were of his own proportion. Psychologists say it is not unusual for a person of such freakish abnormality to fantasize of a world where others are like them, and Gulliver was never able to provide any evidence of his fanciful story.

Apparently tired of being alone, Gulliver returned to Lilliput several years later and sought the favor of the emperor by offering to join the Lilliputian All-Island Olympic Team in its quadrennial events against Blefuscu. His triumphs eclipsed all records and made The Emperor extremely proud. He achieved gold medals in the long jump, the high jump, the 100- and 200-meter sprints, the 1,500-meter run, the discus, and the javelin. In fact, Mr. Gulliver received gold medals in all non-equestrian events.

Having retired from sports, Gulliver married our own Stranamal Redresel and went into the construction business. Longtime business partner Leskul Newportein said of Mr. Gulliver: "He was a great man and a great partner in the construction business. We'll really miss him. Now we'll have to buy a crane."

Mr. Gulliver died in his sleep. His wife survives him, largely because they had no children.

121

3 GHOSTBUSTERS MISSING, PRESUMED DEAD

FAIL TO RETURN FROM ROUTINE ASSIGNMENT IN AMITYVILLE

Mina Harker Diary, April 1, 2015

Dear Diary,

The Count is gone for good. His craving affected his judgment and led to the feeding that would end him.

I telepathically tracked him to Rome. He had snuck into the Vatican Library, posing as an historian of the Church in Transylvania. He hid in the tombs, then made his way through the halls of the Vatican.

Shortly after midnight, he found his quarry and partook of the ultimate meal.

Note to Vampires: If you thought Holy Water burns, try feeding on the Pope!

OP-ED

To the Editor:

I was deeply saddened to read about the loss of one of my beloved fellow vampires, Barnabas Collins. It was particularly painful to discover that the cause of his demise was that pesky Slayer from Sunnydale, Buffy.

We've all dealt with Slayers before, and we know they are just a part of death. But this young woman is nothing but a nuisance. She relishes in disposing the damned for no reason other than to keep us from killing and taking the souls of a few people here and there.

What is most galling are the lies she conjures in order to rally her little band of troublemakers. Why would vampires and demons conspire to rule the world? We already do!

Our dear sweet Barnabas was reconjuring himself from a trip back to the 1870s. He'd made a quick and harmless jaunt back in time to pick up a pair of trousers he'd left on a previous trip. As soon as he had taken shape, this woman, silver bullet at the ready, shot him dead. And this in California! You call this gun control?

It's time we do something. Please contact your coven representatives and ask them to come up with necessary resources and some sort of plan to rid ourselves of this post-pubescent menace.

Yours in sorrow,
Iggy Pop

Lecter's Restaurant

Prix Fixe Tasting Menu

— Chianti —

— Fava Beans —

— Liver a la Clarice —

Come Back to Lecter's—We Love Having Old Friends for Dinner

Hat and Flashlight Found But No Leads on Montgomery College Students Yet

BURKITTSVILLE, Md. (AP) — There are still no clues as to the whereabouts of three filmmakers who hiked into the Black Hills Forest to document the legend of the Blair Witch. Sheriff Ron Cravens said that a hat and flashlight, which may have belonged to Heather Donahue, Joshua Leonard, or Michael Williams, were found by hikers in the woods of North Central Maryland.

Montgomery College film studies chair Ron Geraldi had grave concerns for the students. "These were not the brightest bulbs in the pack, if you know what I mean. I doubt that any of them could follow a map. And God only knows what kind of movie they think they're making. It's been overcast for days. The lighting is terrible. And I know for a fact that none of them know how to use a camera. If they ever do make it back with any footage, I'm sure none of it will be useable."

DING DONG!
WITCH DEAD; WHICH OLD WITCH?

(SEE PAGE 21)

124

STATE OF CALIFORNIA EXECUTES TABITHA STEPHENS

LOS ANGELES, Calif. (*Los Angeles Times*) — In its 40th consecutive month without rainfall, a desperate state took desperate measures to stop the drought that is destroying it. A confused and frustrated populace has watched farms fail, local businesses close, and Los Angeles itself all but shut down.

While scientists point to changing global climate as the cause, the growing popular sentiment has laid the blame on one person: KLXA Los Angeles weatherwoman Tabitha Stephens.

Sacramento farmer Samuel Parris echoes the prevailing sentiment: "Global warming couldn't do this. This is the work of Satan. Her predictions have been perfect 'No Precipitation.' Every night for three years. That's too perfect! And when you play the forecast backward, you can see her nose twitch!"

Last week, Ms. Stephens lost her appeal to the U.S. Supreme Court when it ruled that "Burning at the stake, while cruel and unusual for humans, is perfectly acceptable for witches." Yesterday, the execution took place at the Hollywood Bowl, with over 90,000 in attendance.

"This execution harkens back to a dark and dangerous time in our nation's history. The notion of someone practicing witchcraft in this day and age is preposterous," said Ms. Stephens's attorney, Kevin Lomax.

Ms. Stephens will not require burial.

Mittens Don't Fit, So Jury Acquits

CHICAGO (*Chicago Tribune*, October 3, 1973) — Buffalo Bills star running back O. J. Simpson has been found not guilty of the murder of Bad, Bad Leroy Brown. The jury took less than four hours to reach a unanimous decision in the trial that has gripped America for the last several months.

Mr. Simpson was in Chicago last November for a football game between the Bills and the Chicago Bears. Witnesses at the bar testified that Mr. Brown was messin' with Doris, Mr. Simpson's date, causing the football star to fly into a rage.

Leroy Brown, known by many as the baddest man in the whole damn town of Chicago, was killed in the ensuing struggle. A feared fighter, the 6'4" Mr. Brown proved no match for the star football athlete, who witnesses said was handy with a knife.

Prosecutors and the public were surprised by the verdict. Mr. Simpson's legal team included four Harvard law professors, five Supreme Court justices, and the entire cast of *Dragnet*. Jurors interviewed after the verdict said they just couldn't envision Mr. Simpson wearing the pair of fur mittens that was central to the prosecutor's case. Juror #5 said: "I was willing to believe he would wear that type of mitten, but he'd never get that string up through his sleeves, around his neck, and down the other side. It just wouldn't fit!"

Simpson insisted from the start he was "absolutely, 100 percent not guilty." Mr. Simpson said that he is relieved that this ordeal is over and looks forward to resuming a normal life. And with that, he got into his White Ford Bronco and drove off.

Ashley Madison

"LIFE IS SHORT. HAVE AN AFFAIR."

CHEATING FAQ #7

Q: What can I do to avoid being caught by my spouse?

A: Mix up your pattern. Let's take the case of some fellow I know and Mrs. Jones. They would meet every day at the same cafe, usually around 6:30. Stupid! It wasn't long before Mr. Jones found out and waited for them with a shotgun!

MRS. JONES, 44
No Longer Anything Going On

Bob & Carol & Ted & Alice Die of Consummation

LAS VEGAS (AP) — Calling it one of the most disturbing cases he'd ever seen, the Las Vegas coroner is investigating the deaths of four elderly people at the Kinsey Hotel & Casino on the Strip. The resort, aimed at those nostalgic for the "free love" movement of the 1960s, has attracted thousands of would-be swingers and, according to management, is booked "up the wazoo." Brochures advertise the hotel as "Where Woodstock meets water park—only that's not water!"

Friends say the couples embarked on a journey to fulfill a fantasy 40 years in the making. They scored some Cialis and flew to Vegas. The couples had reserved the Masters and Johnson Suite.

Their bodies were discovered the following morning by housekeeping.

Sgt. Biff Mandalay was first to arrive at the scene. "At first, I thought there had been some sort of horrific murder using a game of Twister," he said. "The bodies were a jumble of limbs and gray hair. On one night table, I saw a wine bottle dripping with candle wax next to a bottle of Advil. On the other was the AARP edition of the Kama Sutra. That's when I realized they were sexual positions."

Unlike the deceased, authorities are tight-lipped about the matter. "What happens in Vegas stays in Vegas," said the coroner. "But jeez, these people are in their seventies! When are the Boomers gonna realize they ain't got it no more?"

As soon as the twisted wreckage of the sexual revolution is dismantled, the embarrassed children of the "generation that would never die" will take their parents home for burial.

MR. SUMMERS

July 1

Fellow citizens. You should all get your silos ready for another bumper crop of grain come September thanks to last week's outstanding sacrifice. The boys gathered a fantastic collection of stones, and the marksmanship exhibited by our citizens has never been better. We'd better be careful or some of our young men are going to go off and pitch for the Red Sox!

I'd like to offer my personal thanks to Tessie Hutchinson, the winner of this year's lottery. Didn't she do a great job! I know some people were a little disappointed at all the bobbing and weaving Tess threw in, but I believe the extra challenge of hitting a moving target just makes the sacrifice more worthy. Of course, I'd also like to offer a shout-out to Bill Hutchinson and the kids.

So, get those tractors ready. And remember, registration for next year's lottery is due by December 31!

Yours in worship,
Lottery Official Summers

SCARLETT O'HARA, 86

Went Hungry Again

ATLANTA (*Atlanta Journal-Constitution*) — Katie Scarlett O'Hara Hamilton Kennedy Butler has died of malnutrition at her antebellum home in Atlanta. Servants reported that Miss O'Hara perished after her stubborn refusal to eat "food made by a Yankee." Her sister, Sister Carreen, had recently hired a cook from Boston to run the kitchen at Tara.

The emaciated O'Hara, who was known to have a shapely 19-inch waist in her twenties, was thinner than pancake batter on a griddle and with about as much sizzle. Her fiery temper and hatred of the North never faltered. She told the *Atlanta Journal-Constitution* last year that "Me and my kind never cared much for Mr. Lincoln, no way, no how, and your Uncle Remus can kiss my grits!"

With her colorful language and piercing glance gone forever, we find ourselves giving a damn.

THE BRITISH DAILY JOURNAL

EDITOR'S NOTE:

We apologize for the delay in publishing an obituary for Philip "Pip" Pirrip, who died last week at 66. The *Journal* approached Mr. Charles Dickens, Pip Pirrip's biographer, about crafting a brief homage to the celebrated businessman. The author insisted that because of the magnitude of the task, the obituary would have to be serialized over the next 26 weeks, with each installment no less than 50,000 words. As Mr. Dickens is paid two pence a word and the publisher is willing to expend only so much for an obituary, the author's expectations will not be fulfilled. Instead, we asked a copy boy to complete the task.

PHILIP (PIP) PIRRIP, 66

The orphan, who rose to prominence and survived life's ups and downs, has died. He leaves a wife, Estella, and two stepchildren. Funeral at a quarter past ten in the churchyard. Burial will be swift.

HOLDEN CAULFIELD, 66

Died in Amusement Park

RYE, N.Y. (AP) — Holden Caulfield, 66, of Long Island City, N.Y., died at Playtime Amusement Park on Monday morning. He was the day's first customer on Playtime's newest ride, "The Cliff," which treats bungee-strapped patrons to a 100-foot drop, after which the rider is caught by an inflatable catcher's mitt. Apparently, amusement park workers had deflated the mitt while doing maintenance on the ride Sunday night. The 66-year-old died instantly upon impact. Park managers are reviewing maintenance procedures with the carnies.

Caulfield was hospitalized for most of the 1960s because of various anxiety disorders. Loner Mark David Chapman stalked him until Caulfield requested a restraining order. That did not stop Chapman from mailing letters and drawings to Caulfield from his prison cell.

The reclusive "auteur of angst" had just completed his memoir *Antihero, My Ass!* and was scheduled to begin a book tour on Monday. The tour will be completed by Caulfield's friend, Alexander Portney. Portney and Caulfield were coauthors of last year's bestseller *Circle Jerks*.

Caulfield is survived by a beloved sister, Phoebe, of Basking Ridge, N.J., and his toy poodle, Stradlater. The Caulfield family requests that no donations be made in Holden's name to his alma mater, Pencey Prep School, because of the fact that the people there are stuck-up and phony.

NEWS REPORTER'S REMAINS FOUND

GUANTANAMO BAY, Cuba (*Washington Post*) — A senior Joint Task Force Guantanamo official has disclosed that human remains have been discovered during the cleanup of Camp X-Ray at Guantanamo Bay. The report was independently confirmed by our source within the FBI, "Sweet Throat."

Originally believed to be the remains of one of the detainees, officials were shocked to discover that the body was that of a woman. Our sources now confirm that the remains are those of television news investigative reporter Murphy Brown.

Brown, news anchor for CBS's *FYI*, had been missing since December 2005 after a particularly harsh piece on the chairman of the FCC. Brown was reported missing by her *FYI* producer Miles Silverberg when she failed to show up for an interview with Rush Limbaugh. "Murphy miss an opportunity to tear Rush a new one? I knew she was dead!"

District police went to Brown's apartment. Although there were no signs of forced entry, there was evidence the Brown had left abruptly. Detective McCarthy explained, "She left her purse, keys, everything. On the kitchen table, there was a plate full of food containing roasted quail, broccoli, and a potato."

The FBI lists Brown as a missing person. The CIA position is that she has probably gone back to drinking. It denies any knowledge of found human remains, a place called "Guantanamo," or Cuba itself.

Social Register

December 4, 1984

WINSTON SMITH

The Ministry of Love is pleased to announce that Mr. Winston Smith, 47, a clerk in the Ministry of Truth, has successfully completed his re-education. Congratulations, Winston!

EPILOGUE

A s he left the card game, Mr. Pilkington seemed to have a brief word with one of the rats. In fact, they had spoken before. Mr. Pilkington had been helping the rats start a new endeavor on the Animal Farm, an oil field. The field proved very profitable, and the rats were able to keep Napoleon in the finest whiskey, tobacco, and clothing.

The rats also used the oil profits to bring creature comforts to the rest of the animals. The cows were given extra hay, and the horses new blankets. And, most importantly, the dogs were given shiny new spike-studded collars. The dogs loved them, and kept asking for new collars with larger spikes, which the rats would gladly provide.

As the years passed, the dogs' interest in Napoleon and Squealer waned, and they spent more and more time with the rats. One day, the dogs came to Pinkeye and told him that he had been working very hard tasting Napoleon's food and should have an evening off. That night, Napoleon fell violently ill, and he died the next day.

Mr. Pilkington stopped by to offer his condolences and invited the rats to the next card game.

Dear Diary,

I spent the day here at Godot's funeral. It was very sad, and we will all miss our good friend very much. I can't even see his face clearly anymore. Estragon was in his usual foul mood, until Pogo and Lucky showed up to distract him. I was expecting more people, but it was only the four of us.

The funeral was to be held at 11:00 a.m. But by 1:00 p.m. the casket had not arrived. I'm certain we were at the right plot—the one by the tree. We didn't see anyone else in the entire cemetery, so this had to be the place. We considered hanging ourselves but didn't want to upstage Godot's final day and decided to do nothing.

By nightfall, we were all hungry. Pogo had his meal but offered none. Near 10:00 p.m., a boy showed up and told us that the funeral has been rescheduled for tomorrow.

We're all going to leave. Soon.

Vladimir

GIANT DEAD BUG GOES ON DISPLAY IN VIENNA

Family Found Insect in Bedroom

Etymologists to Study Intently

VIENNA (AP) — The Samsa family has rented a space at Vienna's Sommerkarneval sideshow to display an enormous beetle, nearly the size of a full-grown man. The thousands of people paying a two-krone admission fee have lifted the Samsas out of poverty.

Grete Samsa said the grotesquely large beetle was found in the bed once occupied by her brother, Gregor, a traveling salesman. Gregor hasn't been seen since the discovery of the gigantic insect. His father believes the young man, who had become a financial burden on the family, may have found a purpose in life and decided to flee. "He probably went through some kind of personal metamorphosis," sighed Mr. Samsa. "Or," Grete opined, "maybe Gregor just went into another state."

The family plans to dress the bug in one of Gregor's old suits and take the oddity on a 22-city tour as part of a traveling circus. Even freak-show veterans are shocked. After seeing the exhibit, Jojo the Dog-Faced Boy said it was "very Kafkaesque."

CLOUSEAU MANSERVANT CATO FOUND DEAD IN REFRIGERATOR

TOULOUSE, France (*Le Monde*) — The skeletal remains of housekeeper and personal martial arts trainer Cato were found in the country home of Inspector Jacques Clouseau. He'd apparently died of suffocation.

The cottage sat abandoned for five years after Clouseau's death from a dog bite. The new owners were startled when they opened the refrigerator and found the intrepid Cato still poised in "attack position."

ARGUMENT BETWEEN BUSINESS PARTNERS LEADS TO FATAL SHOOTING

INDIAN TASKED WITH DOING ALL THE WORK AT KIMOSABE CASINO RESORT KILLED BY MASKED MAN

OBJECTED TO NICKNAME "CHIEF BOTTLE WASHER"

TONTO WAS 57

Inigo Montoya, 50
Unprepared to Die

FLORIN, Italy (IPS) — Inigo Montoya, master swordsman and personal guard to Princess Buttercup and Prince Westley, was killed in a surprise attack by a seven-fingered young man.

Born in Spain, Montoya famously killed Count Rugen in revenge for Rugen's killing of Montoya's father. Now, Count Rugen II has avenged his own father's murder by slaying Montoya. Rugen II's current whereabouts are unknown.

Montoya is survived by his son, Arturo, who is pretty angry about his father's killing.

INDIANA JONES, 72

Swashbuckling Explorer and Archaeologist Survived Large Rolling Balls, Snakes, Nazis, and Poison-Tipped Darts

Dies after Slip and Fall in Shower

Two Wild and Crazy Guys Perish during Grand Opening Event

Festrunk Brothers Smothered in Breasts

MOOREHEAD CITY, N.C. (UPI) — Georg and Yortuk Festrunk, the Czech brothers known as the swingingest bachelors in their adopted country of America, died at the grand opening of their 21st Honkers Bar & Restaurant. The chain's motto is "Home of the Big American Chicken Breasts."

Known for its "Foxily Foxy Foxes," and bartenders sporting crispy chest hairs protruding from their nylon disco shirts, Honkers quickly captured the imagination of American men. Their book *How to Score with the American Foxes and Produce Swinging to the Maximum* was a bestseller in the restaurant gift shop.

The highlight of the evening was to be the brothers' famous "death-defying" stunt in which they are submerged in a tank of their most popular heart-healthy appetizer, the "American Nacho Orgy." The two men lie in the bottom of a tank and are layered with 2,500 pounds of fried chicken cutlets, melted jack cheese, ranch dressing, sour cream, mayonnaise, bacon bits, blue cheese, cheddar cheese, and honey-bourbon sauce.

After several minutes had passed and George and Yortuk failed to emerge from the tank, an assistant manager called the manager at home and asked what to do. It was too late. Firefighters took 10 hours to collect evidence in 6,000 Ziploc bags, requiring three separate trips to the station house freezer. After hosing down the victims, investigators realized the men's numerous gold chains had become entangled in each other's flailing arms and thwarted their escape.

In accordance with their will, the Festrunks' bodies will be flown to the Bahamas and buried in a double plot near Anna Nicole Smith.

ARNOLD ZIFFEL, 35

UNOFFICIAL "MAYOR" OF HOOTERVILLE

HOOTERVILLE — Arnold Ziffel, who embraced the title of "pig" with gusto, died at the Hooterville Old Pigs Retirement Home, surrounded by hooters of various sizes. Many had come to his bedside from Petticoat Junction to be with the accomplished porker as he held court one last time, dressed in silk pajamas and smoking a pipe.

A frequenter of the bar and restaurant chain that he started right here in his hometown, Arnold enjoyed hooters young and old, wherever they may be: in the "sty" (his crib), around the swimming pool, in church, and out in public.

Ziffel was an accomplished painter, who often incorporated hooters into his oils. Many of the paintings were sold to bachelor pigs, which enjoyed seeing the hooters hang prominently in their bedrooms. For pigs that love hooters, the bigger the better, so Arnold made sure to exaggerate them for greater effect. His muse was Oliver Wendell Douglas's exotic wife, Lisa, whose accent, and especially her mammoth hooters, made him snort lustfully. This was a true pig here.

In his illustrious career, Arnold attempted to mate with pretty much anything that had a pulse, including Mr. Haney's basset hound. They did not produce a litter, but in doing so, Arnold cemented his reputation as a true pig. He seemed to have a never-ending pen of pendulous playmates at his beck and call.

Arnold's death also brings to an end the rumor that the cast and crew of a sitcom shot in the town of Hooterville ate Arnold at the wrap party. The truth is that residents of the town roasted the basset hound over a spit and told the Hollywood visitors it was pork.

JOEY TRIBBIANI, 47
Game Show Host, Actor

LIVINGSTON, N.J. (*The Star Ledger*) — Joey Tribbiani was shot and killed today inside the home of his former roommate Chandler Bing. Mr. Bing is being held by the Livingston police pending charges of murder. Police report that Mr. Bing flew into a jealous rage upon returning home from a business trip and finding Mr. Tribbiani in his home visiting Mrs. Monica Geller-Bing. Mr. Tribbiani was declared dead at the scene.

Mr. Tribbiani's career started with a role as Dr. Drake Ramoray in *Days of our Lives*, where he appeared on and off for over 10 years. In a highly controversial move, Tribbiani was selected to replace Alex Trebek as the host of *Jeopardy!* upon Mr. Trebek's retirement. Intended to appeal to a younger audience, the experiment lasted only one show when Mr. Tribbiani clashed with the show's judges. Outraged over what he felt was an unfair ruling, Tribbiani sided with a contestant arguing that a pound of feathers could not possibly weigh as much as a pound of lead. He was replaced by Jessica Simpson.

Mr. Tribbiani's big break came when he became the host of what would become America's number one reality show, *Tattoo This*. Tribbiani was both the host and creator of the show, in which contestants compete for the right to select the type and location of a tattoo to be placed on the loser. It was the first show to top *American Idol* in over a decade. Tribbiani said the idea came to him when he was forced to get a tattoo after losing a bet concerning who is buried in Lenin's Tomb (hint: It isn't one of the Beatles).

Neighbors of the Bings report that Mr. Bing was an advertising executive and traveled often on business. Mr. Tribbiani was a frequent visitor during those times. But, according to police, Mrs. Bing claims there was no inappropriate relationship between her and Mr. Tribbiani and that they were just Friends.

ALMOST

EVERYBODY
LOVES RAYMOND

Sportswriter Found
Bludgeoned with
Baseball Bat

(See page 27)

MIAMI HERALD

4 Golden Girls Found Dead on Newly Waxed Kitchen Floor

FELL AND COULDN'T GET UP

CBS Announces Cast Changes on Saturday Morning Cartoons

PHOENIX, Ariz. (UPI) — CBS Executives chose this southwest location to announce major changes to some of its most popular shows:

On the *Road Runner Show*, Wile E. Coyote will retire from his role of the long-suffering antagonist to be replaced by Predator.

In *Tweety Bird Cartoons*, Sylvester the Cat will be joined by the more accomplished combatant, Alien.

CBS Spokesman explained the decisions. "Let's face it, Wyle E. is never going to catch Road Runner, and Sylvester is never going to eat Tweety Bird. We all know that. We believe these changes will open up new story lines and provide fresh challenges for these famously evasive birds."

VARIETY

ROAD RUNNER CARTOON SHOW CANCELLED AFTER NEW SEASON'S FIRST EPISODE

Network executives announced the cancellation of the Road Runner cartoon show due to the death of Mr. Road Runner. Fans will be disappointed to learn that the final show lasts only 27 seconds.

The cartoon company had been highly optimistic about the new fall season with the introduction of new cast member, famed hunter Predator.

One critic who attended the screening described the action: "The intro song starts playing. The title is displayed. This episode is called "Road Kill." This takes about 15 seconds. Road Runner comes zooming down the road from miles away, leaving a trail of dust. He passes behind a mountain, then comes into screen and stops suddenly at a mound of bird feed in the middle of the road. That is when Predator blasts him with a plasma gun. A small wisp of smoke slowly dissipates from where the bird had been standing. That's it."

The show's producer reflected on the turn of events. "Predator definitely livened up the show. But in retrospect, perhaps he was not a good fit with Road Runner. We're looking for other opportunities that might make better use of his extreme and unrelenting style of fighting. We're in talks with people over at *Desperate Housewives*."

Canary Conquers Alien Assassin

HUNTINGTON, Calif. (*Los Angeles Times*) — Los Angeles police, responding to a call for help, came upon a gruesome triple murder. Police identified the victims as the owner of the house, Granny, her dog, Hector, and her cat, Sylvester.

Police identified the murderer as Alien, the infamous Xenomorph that has tormented space travelers for decades. The buglike creature had come to L.A. in response to an ad in the "Murder for Hire" section of craigslist. Records show the ad had been placed by Mr. Sylvester.

According to the sole surviving member of the household, Tweety Bird, the problems began when Alien came to stay in their house two weeks ago. Granny, accepting the creature as a guest of her cat, originally consented to the arrangement. But as Alien became more and more aggressive toward her beloved Tweety, she took matters into her own hands and tried to throw the Alien out. Pan, broom, and bulldog proved little match for the accomplished killer, and they were ripped to pieces.

Inexplicably, the Alien then turned on its employer, Sylvester, and held the cat in place as its acidic fluids consumed the cat's flesh. Terrified, the canary retreated to its birdcage.

Alien pushed a wooden ladder over to the cage and started to ascend, not realizing he'd placed it in the pool of acid. Just as Tweety was shouting "I did! I did! I did see an Alien," the ladder disintegrated.

Alien was slammed against an ironing board cabinet, cracking its exoskeleton. With poor eyesight, Alien did not notice the iron slowly sliding down the board until it scorched its tail.

Shocked by the pain, Alien's limbs shot out in all directions, its claws sticking into two mousetraps, a toaster, and an electrical outlet. With the toaster and the electrical outlet on the same circuit, the creature was quickly electrocuted and reduced to charred rubble. That is when Tweety placed the call to 911.

143

SMARTWOOL ALUMNI BLOG

TWINS REUNITED IN DEATH
SOCK PUPPET MURDER-SUICIDE DEVASTATES FAMILY DRAWER

The popular Pets.com Sock Puppet was killed yesterday by a long-lost brother with whom he was recently reunited.

The pair had been separated nearly eight years ago at a Laundromat in Silicon Valley. The brother had been statically bound to a pair of extra-large woman's panties and packed into the bag of a female tourist returning to Latvia. Once unpacked, he was quickly tossed into the garbage but managed to escape and went on to become a Spokes-Sock Puppet for the Zelta beer brand.

The Pets.com Sock Puppet searched for his brother in vain. Experts say that pairs of socks who are separated usually die within 48 hours. That both brothers survived and went on to similar careers is considered amazing.

The brothers were reunited when they ran into each other at a Sock Puppet branding conference in Las Vegas. By coincidence, Mr. Pets and Mr. Zelta were speakers on the same panel: "Coping With an Overly Controlling Hand." Mr. Pets immediately invited his brother to move in with him at his Santa Barbara estate.

Although the Pets.com company was one of the most famous Dot Bombs, the sock puppet had done well. While publicly promoting the company as its mascot, privately, Mr. Pets was taking huge short positions in its stock. The bankruptcy made him a multimillionaire.

Mr. Pets was convicted of insider trading. But that conviction was overturned by the Ninth Circuit Court of Appeals when they ruled that SEC rules do not apply to puppets, citing *United States v. Lamb Chop*.

At first, it was a joyous reunion. Mr. Pets treated his brother to several cosmetic darnings, the finest fabric softeners, and gave him his own drawer in which to sleep. But Mr. Zelta grew jealous and bitter over the life he had been denied.

Police say that yesterday, Mr. Zelta finally snapped. Mr. Pets had taken a bath and was in the dryer when Mr. Zelta blocked the door, turned the heat to "max," and let it run for hours. Mr. Pets, with 20 percent nylon, melted into a shriveled rag. Mr. Zelta called the police himself, but refused to surrender. After a five-hour standoff, he attached one of his threads to the moisture sensor button, jumped off the dryer, and completely unraveled.

Services will be presided over by the Right Reverend Triumph the Insult Comic Dog.

Serial abuser has thrown last punch

DOMESTIC VIOLENCE CLAIMS LIFE OF ABUSIVE PUPPET AT LOCAL THEATER

Punch's Piercing Screams Ignored by Laughing Audience

Judy's Defense: "He Beat Me With Sausage"

Family Excursion Down Winding Beverly Hills Road Turns Disastrous

Millionaire Jed Clampett Shocked to Find Empty Rocking Chair on Truck Roof

Granny, 77, Presumed Dead

Prospecting for Oil with Shotgun, Millionaire Jed Clampett Discovers Natural Gas Deposit

Funeral to be Held Saturday; He was 68

PRAYERS OF THANKS

Thank you, brother Ezekiel, for allowing me to serve justice, smite my enemies, make some serious goddamn cash, and live to tell about it. As I embark on one final score, please watch over me so I do not get my motherf***in' ass shot. Also help me stay focused so I don't try nothin' snaky with Marsellus's hot wife.

> Your humble servant,
> Jules Winnfield
> Ezekiel 25:17

Thank you, Jesus, for allowing me, a most righteous man, to avenge the disrespect laid upon my personage by my (formerly trusted) employee. Not only did his skinny ass try to abscond with 20 kilos of my precious property, but he attempted to covet my lovely wife, Mia, and there ain't no way he lived for more than five seconds to regret it.

> With all praises,
> Marsellus Wallace
> Ezekiel 25:17

FAT LADY SINGS, DIES

Hair, Horns, and High C Attract Hunters

Siegfried Distraught

Warbucks Accidentally Shot Dead by Adopted Daughter while Raiding Her Piggy Bank

Famous for Unabashed War Profiteering; Provided Munitions to Troops

HYDE PARK, N.Y. — A tragic accident has left zillionaire Oliver Warbucks dead. His adopted daughter Annie, alerted by her trusty dog Sandy to a sudden noise, shot her daddy late last night.

Annie, who could not see very well in the dark because of the absence of eyes, kept a gun by her bed in case Nazi spies skulked around the Warbucks estate. Thinking the bald-headed Warbucks was a helmeted German, the curly-haired lass pulled a Luger P08 and shot him. Warbucks was found dead, clutching the young girl's piggybank.

A broken piggy bank containing $3.12 has been taken by police as evidence.

As he had done many times before, the richest man in America had returned from one of his lengthy business trips penniless. In times past, he had raided Annie's piggy bank but always returned the money once he'd made another zillion dollars. Somehow, this seemed to be a credible business practice to Warbucks's investors. His rising and falling fortunes never appeared to be a cause for concern to bankers or government officials with whom he did business.

Oliver Warbucks's assistant, Earl P. Halliburton, will assume the presidency of Warbucks Industries.

ROLL OF DICE IN REAL ESTATE SCHEME SENDS RICH UNCLE PENNYBAGS TO DEBTOR'S PRISON

WENT TO JAIL, DIRECTLY TO JAIL, DID NOT PASS GO, AND DID NOT COLLECT $200

PEDESTRIAN CUISINE IN PRISON SICKENS MR. MONOPOLY; WAS 84

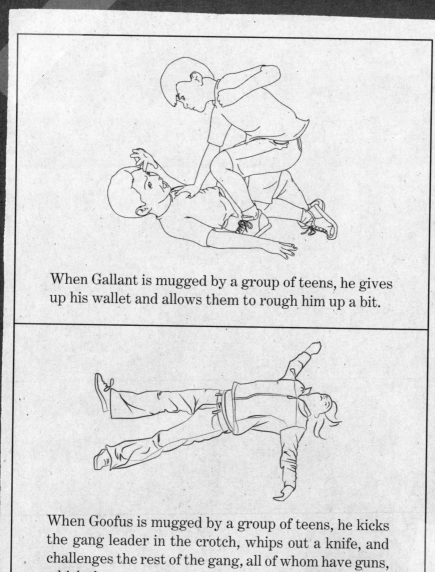

When Gallant is mugged by a group of teens, he gives up his wallet and allows them to rough him up a bit.

When Goofus is mugged by a group of teens, he kicks the gang leader in the crotch, whips out a knife, and challenges the rest of the gang, all of whom have guns, which they use without hesitation.

LITTLE BOY BLEW

CITY OF PAMPLONA MOURNS GORED TEENAGER, 17

The Sheep Were in the Meadow, the Cows in the Corn, and the Bull, Unfortunately, Was Five Feet Away

PAMPLONA, Spain (*El Correo Tiempo*) — José Maria Ibarra Etxeberria Garcia Varga, bugle player and apprentice shepherd, has died from wounds inflicted by an angry bull Tuesday afternoon.

The bleary-eyed youngster had not noticed that a bull had wandered into his yard. In typical teen fashion, the velvet-clad child was snoozing under a pile of hay in a wagon instead of working. Upon awakening, José blew his bugle to call in the flocks of sheep, enraging the bull.

A chase ensued through the heart of the city. José was joined by tens, then hundreds, of reckless, hormone-riddled young men who joined the run, thinking it a game of machismo. The streets of Pamplona were thrust into complete confusion and chaos, as rapt city dwellers cheered the boys on.

His progress impeded by the exhilarated throng, José was eventually cornered and gored by the bull.

Traditionally, when a matador kills a bull, the testicles are breaded, fried, and served to the mayor. The mayor of Pamplona expressed concern about what's for dinner when the bull wins.

CAPTAIN MORGAN, 170

THE CARIBBEAN (AP) — Spice Boy and renowned party buccaneer Captain Morgan was killed yesterday in a confrontation with the Coast Guard. The Master Mixologist's ship, the *Blender*, was pulled over by Coast Guard Cutter USS *Teetotaler* when it was observed weaving in and out of shipping lanes. A Coast Guard spokesman reports that the initial stop was for suspicion of SWI (Swashbuckling While Intoxicated). He was 170 years old and was considered well-preserved for his age.

The USCG reports that Morgan initially tried to outrun the cutter. But the 17th-century schooner had little success evading the 17,000 horsepower military vessel. The captain's ship was quickly captured and boarded. Drunk out of his mind, Morgan swore to expel the raiders and threw a rum punch.

Morgan was shot 17 times. Rum spewed from every bullet hole, which was caught in flagons and quaffed by the grog-deprived seaman. They reported being happy that they had a little Captain Morgan in them.

As per his standing orders, Captain Morgan was buried at sea by his crew. In lieu of a wreath, the spot was marked by tub of ice, 17 gallons of fruit punch, and a large umbrella.

GIN GAME TURNS TRAGIC

JIM BEAM ICED DURING CARD GAME

MOUNT GAY, Belize (UPI) — The Grand Marnier of Belize announced this morning at a press conference that several guests of Tia Maria's Canadian Club were taken to St. Pauli Girl Hospital after a card game went awry.

Details are sketchy, but a witness said that after being dealt a particularly bad hand of gin, Jack Daniels tossed his cards down and called the dealer, José Cuervo, a beefeater. That made José's longtime companion, Johnny Walker, red. Walker threw a punch and instead struck Jim Beam in the temple. Beam's girlfriend, Blackberry Brandy, put him on ice while waiting for EMTs to arrive.

Sam Buca and Glen Fiddich, the club's bouncers, ejected the remaining pugilistic boilermakers. They were whiskeyed off to the tanq, where they spent the night in southern comfort until Bailey Fran Gelico escorted them to arraignment before a bitter Judge Angu Stora.

Jim Beam was reportedly extremely drambuie on the way to the hospital and later died—but not before giving Brandy his Bombay sapphire ring. Entertainer Smirnoff Blue, an orthodox Jew, said Chivas for the victim.

Remy Martin, the highball Courvoisier of Belize, later tried to reassure tourists that the resort is perfectly safe—an absolut crown royal place to vacation.

153

Malibu Police Department Investigation Report
MPD-1157/22

LOCATION OF INCIDENT:
PACIFIC COAST HIGHWAY

DESCRIPTION OF INCIDENT:
WHITE MALE, MID-TO-LATE 40S. FOUND DEAD IN CAR ON SIDE OF PCH.

VICTIM LAST NAME:	FIRST NAME:
HARPER	CHARLIE

DA'S FILE NUMBER:	ASSIGNED TO:
287937	DETECTIVE RICHARD VAUGHN

DISPOSITION:
RULED ACCIDENTAL DEATH BY PRIAPISM.

DESCRIPTION OF EVIDENCE:
PRESCRIPTION BOTTLE OF CIALIS FILLED IN THE NAME OF VICTIM ON DAY OF INCIDENT. 8 PILLS MISSING.

TIMELINE:
WITNESS STATEMENTS ACCOUNT FOR THE LAST 4.5 HOURS PRIOR TO DEATH.

WITNESS STATEMENTS:

WITNESS NAME:	RELATIONSHIP:
ALAN HARPER	BROTHER

STATEMENT:
CHARLIE GOT BACK FROM THE PHARMACY ABOUT 6:30 AND SAID HE HAD A BIG NIGHT PLANNED. HE GOT ALL DRESSED UP IN HIS TIGHTEST JEANS BUT WENT BACK TO HIS ROOM TO PUT ON SOME LOOSE-FITTING SWEAT PANTS. THAT WAS UNUSUAL FOR A NIGHT OUT.

WITNESS NAME:	RELATIONSHIP:
MISTY	"ESCORT"

STATEMENT:
I SAW CHARLIE AT ABOUT 6, AND HE WAS FINE.

154

WITNESS NAME:	RELATIONSHIP:
DESTINY	"ESCORT"

STATEMENT:
CHARLIE CAME BY AT 7; WE HAD A GREAT TIME.

WITNESS NAME:	RELATIONSHIP:
CANDY	"ESCORT"

STATEMENT:
I WAS SUPPOSED TO MEET CHARLIE AT 8. I WAS CONCERNED BECAUSE HE WAS A LITTLE LATE. HE'S NEVER LATE. BUT HE WAS READY TO GO WHEN HE GOT HERE.

WITNESS NAME:	RELATIONSHIP:
TIFFANY	"ESCORT"

STATEMENT:
CHARLIE DIDN'T GET HERE UNTIL 9:30. HE LOOKED PRETTY BAD. I TOLD HIM I HAD ANOTHER DATE AT 10:00, BUT HE DIDN'T SEEM TO MIND. WHEN HE WAS LEAVING, I ASKED HOW LONG HE'D BEEN LIKE THAT. I TOLD HIM AFTER 4 HOURS, YOU'RE SUPPOSED TO CALL YOUR DOCTOR, BUT HE SAID HE HAD ONE MORE STOP.

WITNESS NAME:	RELATIONSHIP:
YVETTE	"ESCORT"

STATEMENT:
YEAH, I WAS SUPPOSED TO SEE CHARLIE, BUT HE NEVER SHOWED. WE HAD A CONFIRMED APPOINTMENT. THAT MEANS HE OWES ME. DO YOU KNOW WHO HIS EXECUTOR IS, HONEY?

POGO, 6

HE MET THE ENEMY, AND IT WAS HIM

Bizarre Nighttime Accident Kills Philosophical Possum

OKEFENOKEE SWAMP (UPI) — Better to let Pogo's friend Churchy LaFemme tell the story: "Well, as I hear it, that ol' boy done woke up after hearin' a noise about his home. Jes' then, he come face to face with a intruder. Was it a commi-nest he was thinkin' or, worse, the ghost of Joe McCarthy?

"Anyways, ol' Pogo don't like the looks of 'em. He pick up a stick and swung hard. Well, his eyes wasn't all that good, 'cause it was a mirror he was swingin' at, jiminy, and it went-a-crashin'.

"Pogo caught a big piece 'o' glass in his juggler vein, and you know the rest. To think that ol' boy ran for pres'dint once! Well, I guess this shows he was dumb 'nough to be pres'dint."

Explosion at Dogpatch Meth Lab Leaves Abner Yokum Dead

Abner "Was 'Vestigatin' a Bubblin' Sound Out Yonder" When Backyard Shack Blew Up, According to Mammy Yokum

Aggrieved Widder Daisy Mae "Ain't Speakin' to No %#*! Press"

Whipple Squeezes; Jealous Husband Questioned for Murder

AKRON, Ohio (AP) — Mr. George Whipple, known to have a lascivious obsession with toilet paper rolls, was found in the trunk of a car destined for compaction at Lou's Scrap Yard. A note found on the body read, "Here's what you get for squeezing Charmaine's rolls, you pervert."

Whipple's neighbor, Gladys Kravitz, called police when she noticed that Whipple's blue frock hung on the clothesline for three and a half days and was on the verge of violating local laundry-hanging ordinances. She peered in every window and didn't see Whipple anywhere—not in his bathroom with the deluxe six-roll dispenser. Not on his easy chair, padded with fresh scent quintuple-ply bathroom tissue. And not even on his bed, made entirely out of toilet paper rolls.

A missing persons alert went out to Akron police, who immediately paid a visit to Lou's, where dozens of other men have been found in car trunks over the years.

Detectives identified four women in a 10-square-mile area named Charmaine and brought their husbands in for questioning. One suspect, 56-year-old Louis Ferraro, is the prime suspect. Police believe a misunderstanding contributed to the killing. Last week, Mr. Ferraro overheard a group of men laughing about Whipple, who had been caught squeezing Charmin in the supermarket. Ferraro, who is hard of hearing, became enraged and drove off.

As requested in his will, Mr. Whipple was bound in Charmin toilet tissue before being flushed into the Ohio River.

MAYTAG REPAIRMAN DEAD

Tired of the Boredom, Took Job with Chinese Manufacturer Shenhua Washing Machine Company

Died at 57 from Exhaustion

157

DR. C. T. PEPPER, 57

DIABETES RESEARCHER, VICTIM OF COLA WARS

ATLANTA, Ga. (AP, September 23, 1910) — The 57-year-old scientist and diabetes expert Dr. C. T. Pepper is being remembered as a courageous crusader against dangerous eating habits.

The good doctor, who invented the sugar-laden digestive elixir that bears his name, experienced a conversion to healthy eating habits after a visit to the Battle Creek Sanitarium. Dr. John Harvey Kellogg's acclaimed holistic center in Battle Creek, Mich., stresses nutrition and exercise as a means to fitness and fine health. This approach is considered quackery by the American Medical Association. It was over a bowl of frosted flakes in the sanitarium that Dr. Pepper had a revelation about the dangers of over-consumption of sugar.

Dr. Pepper presented a damning paper to the AMA titled "What the Hell Is Wrong with You People; Are You Crazy?" In it, he exposed a secret plot by manufacturers to develop an inexpensive sweetener derived from corn that could eventually give everybody in America diabetes.

The paper was roundly criticized by industry fat cats. Promoters of healthy eating rushed to Pepper's defense, including Dr. Kellogg, Heinrich Granola, the Women's Roughage Movement, and the Scottish Steel-Cut Oat Council.

In an act of solidarity, they declared: "You're a Pepper, I'm a Pepper, she's a Pepper, he's a Pepper—wouldn't you like to be a Pepper too?"

Soon, his defenders would be forced underground, as news emerged that Dr. Pepper's sticky body was found at the bottom of a pile of soda bottles in Atlanta.

WORKMEN BLAMED FOR DEATH OF WONKA FACTORY OWNER

LEEDS, England (AP) — Mr. Charles Bucket, president and CEO of Wonka Industries, has died from injuries he received while riding in a glass elevator at the Wonka Chocolate Factory here in Leeds. He was accompanied by three children.

An Oompah Loompah witnessed the accident. It said that Bucket was taking the children for a tour of the grounds, which begins with a ride in a glass elevator at a high rate of speed. Normally, the elevator crashes through the stained glass ceiling of the elevator shaft for dramatic effect.

Tragically, a contractor new to Wonka Industries replaced the glass roof with concrete.

DNA testing is expected to confirm the identity of Mr. Bucket's smithereens, plus those of the three unfortunate children and their Gobstoppers.

New Chocolate Factory CEO Elected

The Wonka board of directors has named a successor; the runner-up in the contest that elevated Mr. Bucket to president. It's heiress and star of the hit British TV series *The Apprentice: Royal Bitch*, the Duchess of Blackwell, Verucà Salt.

Cole Sear, Boy with Sixth Sense, 11

NOW, DEAD PEOPLE SEE HIM

Death, the Scythe-Wielding, Black-Hooded Harbinger of Doom Is Dead

Undiagnosed Nut Allergy

Millions Report Feeling Better

Population Experts Concerned

Death, shown here on his day off

GRASSHOPPER DEAD AT 47

Everybody was Kung Fu Fighting

Master Po: "It was a Little Bit Frightening"

Murder of Kwai Chang Caine was as Fast as Lightning

Beatrix Kiddo Charged; Used Five-Point Palm-Exploding Heart Technique

See Page 4

MAN ON THE STREET

Q: What is the worst thing you have hit with your car?

A: "We thought we felt a bump, you know, like a speed bump, only on one side. I didn't realize there was a race going on. Apparently, we were at the finish line. A few minutes later, a hare showed up and seemed pretty happy, but my wife won't forgive me."

—Farmer Watkins, Derbyshire, recent divorcee

MAN BITES DOG—REALLY!

McGruff the Crime Dog Attacked

LIBERTY CITY, N.J. (AP) — Tragedy struck at the Liberty City Parade on Saturday when a man, foaming at the mouth, attacked McGruff the Crime Dog. Witnesses heard the deranged man scream "I'm gonna take a bite out of you!" before he lunged at the trench-coat-sporting canine. The perpetrator, a resident of Vice City, said that by killing McGruff, he had accomplished the ultimate mission.

As the mortally wounded hound was whisked away to Fort Lee Animal Hospital, chaos ensued. Bullies, petty thieves, prostitutes, and drug offenders cheered. Social mores were abandoned. Rioting gangs burned cars, threw Molotov cocktails, and battered SWAT teams with bottles and rocks.

Hundreds are being charged with grand theft auto. Liberty City is locked down at the borders of Secaucus, Hoboken, Bayonne, and all river crossings. PATH trains are running on a Sunday and holiday schedule.

After being told that the canine crime fighter's treatment would run into hundreds of dollars, the mayor ordered McGruff euthanized.

DEVELOPER DOESN'T GIVE A HOOT FOR WOODSY OWL

TREE-HUGGER FINDS BODY OF ADVERTISING MASCOT CLINGING TO OTHER SIDE OF DOWNED TREE

BEND, Ore. — Environmental icon Woodsy Owl perished in the Deschutes National Forest after his habitat was sold off to a developer with ties to members of Congress. The forest, near Oregon's Cascade Range, had recently been clear-cut as part of the Interior Department's Mother Earth Initiative. An Interior spokeswoman said, "Where do you think we get all that paper pulp to produce those Give a Hoot, Don't Pollute posters?"

The spotted owl was beloved by children, crunchy granola types, and crying Indians. A grieving Smokey Bear tore the heads off two lobbyists standing outside a hearing room, where a congressional panel was due to wring its hands and make supercilious pronouncements about the sad state of affairs surrounding environmental protection. Shortly thereafter, Congress passed Resolution CYA-86, which approves funding to monitor the loss of spotted owls with eyeglasses.

Woodsy will be stuffed, mounted, and displayed at the U.S. Chamber of Commerce.

163

SAM "MAYDAY" MALONE, 65

RED SOX PITCHER, PROPRIETOR

BOSTON (*Boston Globe*) — Sam Malone, a relief pitcher for the Boston Red Sox in the late 1970s until alcoholism drove him from the game, was shot and killed yesterday in a Boston Bordello.

Malone, whose nickname was "Mayday," was best known for his "Slider of Death," although it was unclear whether the accolade was awarded by teammates or opponents.

After leaving baseball, Malone took the unlikely step of opening a bar. He explained to friends that "the best way to deal with your problems is to confront them head-on," and for a while, he succeeded. He called the bar "Cheers: Where Everybody Knows Your Name."

However, what seemed like a good idea at the time eventually led to relapse. Malone said liquor in the bar was not the least bit tempting. What drove him to drink were the patrons. He explained to a sports reporter in 1997: "The pathetic drunk who lived at the bar, the annoying mailman, the stupid bartender, and his even dumber son. Even worse was the pompous psychiatrist who spent way too much time in a bar to be giving anyone advice. And then, of course, there was that bitch I sold the bar to. We should have called it 'Cheers: Where All the Jokes Sound the Same.'"

After another round of rehab, Malone found himself banished from the bar. He started living off credit cards. At first, it was just groceries, then some new furniture for the apartment, then a new home theater. Soon, Malone's addictive tendency reared its ugly head in the form of spending and

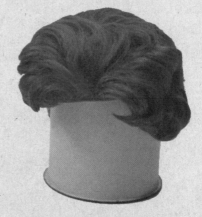

debt. After declaring bankruptcy, Malone completed a program with Debtors Anonymous. A short time later, he parlayed his baseball celebrity into a position as a loan officer with the Citizens Bank of Massachusetts and referred to his group as: "Cheers: Where Credit Cards Are to Blame."

But the work-a-day world left Malone bored and depressed. He soon turned to drugs and quickly acquired a $1,500 a day heroin habit. Again, with the support of friends and yet another trip to rehab, Malone was able to kick it. And just to make sure he stayed off the stuff, Malone opened his own heroin den and prided himself on the attractive décor, good service, and clean needles. He called it "Cheers: Where Everybody Knows Your Vein."

The heroin den was thriving and Malone was confident that he was done with chemical dependencies. But one more peril was looming: Malone's weakness for the ladies.

see Malone Dead, page 35

Finding himself in the presence of young female junkies willing to trade their charms for smack, Malone was soon caught in the rapture of sexual addiction. It wasn't until a bout of hepatitis brought the risks into focus that he was able to conquer his lust. Just to make sure he never faltered in his newfound celibacy, Malone bought back his old bar and turned it into a whorehouse. He called it "Cheers: Where Everybody Knows Your Stain."

Malone was shot after an argument with a john who had refused to pay his tab. He was 65.

LOVE CANAL BARBIE® DEAD AT 42

Consumers Repelled by Features Such As "Skin Lesions and Removable Clumps of Hair"

Collectors Flocking to Auction Web Sites for Deals

MELANOMA CLAIMS LIFE OF COPPERTONE GIRL

She was 45. Her skin was 90.

TEAM MASCOT PUT DOWN BY NTSA AGENTS (MLB)

PHILADELPHIA (AP) — The Philly Phanatic was shot and killed yesterday by security agents at Philadelphia International Airport. Mr. Phanatic, the Phillies Director of Enthusiasm, had arrived at the airport for the team flight to Cincinnati. However, gate agents informed Mr. Phanatic that his highly public phanatical behavior had gotten him placed on the Homeland Security No Phly List.

Outraged, the 6'5" native of the Galapagos started ranting, raving, and rolling around on the floor. Agents advised the Phanatic to moderate his behavior and leave the airport. The Phanatic responded by giving them the "Whammy Hand." When threatened with forced removal, the Phanatic pulled out his Hot Dog Shooter and started spraying the agents with ground pork lips, nitrates, and mustard. The agents returned fire, killing the large green bird thing.

A Phillies spokesman said the team was saddened by the incident. "We relied on the Phanatic to get us going. We thrived on his feigned hostility, and his boisterous, obnoxious behavior." While the Phillies seek a permanent replacement, the position will be filled by Lenny Dykstra.

Major League Baseball Loses Another Mascot, Regains Another Villain

ATLANTA (*Atlanta Journal Constitution*) — The New York Mets' team mascot, Mr. Met, was killed last night in a Peachtree Avenue bar. The jovial cheerleader had gone out for a drink after yesterday's 7–2 loss to the Atlanta Braves. Teammates say it was not uncommon for Mr. Met to go to a bar after a team loss. Often several. He is credited with penning the team's Opening Day motto "There's always next year!"

Mr. Met arrived at The Peach Pitt at approximately 12:30 a.m. and was immediately noticed by former Braves' relief pitcher John Rocker. Rocker soon began to verbally assault Mr. Met, calling him a typical big-headed "New York freak." Rocker grabbed a souvenir bat from the wall and began swinging. In his first two attempts, he failed to connect, but with the count 0–2, he struck Mr. Met in the head. An autopsy report shows that Mr. Met died from the loss of substantial amounts of wool yarn.

The National League stats have been updated to reflect Mr. Rocker's new and improved batting average.

MUDVILLE DISAPPOINTED AGAIN

The outlook wasn't brilliant at Mudville ER that day.
The hero who had led their team may have checked in to stay.
The kidneys didn't seem quite right, the liver nearly shot.
It looked like the mighty Casey had simply gone to pot.

As seems so often was the case when athletes leave the field
Casey had by habits come, that health was not to yield.
And drink and smoke were not alone in the vices Casey chose.
It was in one game long ago that he lost his shirt to Rose.

The doctors summoned to the case were not the best, you know.
Because of Casey's paupered state, he'd joined an HMO.
Fresh and young, just out of school, making their first diagnosis,
The doctors had mixed up the charts and said "It's osteoporosis."

The nurses gasped, the interns sneered, what could these doctors know?
But Casey raised his weakened arm and did forbearance show.

And then one intern found a book and thought perhaps a cure.
With all the weight that Casey gained, they might try Lipitor.
And then the second doctor offered a fresh analysis.
He said, I know, we must right now get this man dialysis.

Casey's prospects still declined, this much is surely true.
His heart stopped cold, his body slumped, and someone called "Code Blue!"
And now the paddles are applied and the doctor presses hard.
And now he pulls the trigger and administers the charge.

Oh, somewhere in this favored land the sun is shining bright,
The band is playing somewhere, and somewhere hearts are light,
And somewhere men are laughing and little children shout;
But there is no joy in Mudville—mighty Casey has checked out.

168

Edward Scissorhands, 57, Dies at Starting Line of Marathon

SALISBURY, Md. (AP) — Edward Scissorhands, whose outré style and bizarre appendages had left him ostracized for nearly a decade, died Monday at the starting line of the Boston Marathon.

Left prehensiley challenged by a careless inventor, Scissorhands' early forays into society were awkward, leading to run-ins with the law and spurning by the community. After gaining employment at the Purdue chicken factory, he angered still more neighbors whose layoffs resulted from his ability to quarter 1,400 birds an hour.

But a near tragedy helped to bring the boy back into society. A serious automobile accident had left several high school students trapped in a car. The fire department's Jaws of Life malfunctioned, making rescue impossible. The captain sent for Scissorhands, who had the teens out within minutes. In appreciation, the town named the new community center after the hero, and he was the guest of honor at the ribbon-cutting ceremony.

Scissorhands found he enjoyed the excitement and service of the rescue. He became an EMT. Once, while attempting to administer CPR, Scissorhands accidentally performed bypass surgery. Fortunately, that was exactly what the patient needed, but the risks to others were too great, and he was reassigned to a desk duty.

Earlier this year, Edward was once again the talk of the town after winning a coveted entry into the Boston Marathon. He trained diligently. Nobody thought to warn Edward of the danger.

The motherless Scissorhands had never heard the adage "Don't run with scissors"!

GREEN GIANT, 54

Valley of the Jolly Giant Sold Off to Developers

Executive Homes to Replace Rolling Fields of Peas, Carrots, and Beans

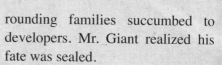

JOLLY VALLEY (AP) — Despondent, depressed, and too large to fit in a homeless shelter, the Green Giant entered a canning facility Wednesday and threw himself into a machine used for creaming corn. A spokesman for Ripham-Downe Developers, Inc., said papers had been passed on the Giant's valley property just a day before the despondent gargantuan shouted "Ho, ho, no!" and dove into Del Monte's Cream-O-Tarium 3000®.

The Giants, the Libbys, the Allens, the Senecas, and the Hunts all had deep roots in this community. Suburban sprawl triggered soaring property values, and one by one, surrounding families succumbed to developers. Mr. Giant realized his fate was sealed.

The Pennsylvania Dutchman mushroom man, a longtime friend, said that Mr. Giant had started hitting the sauce. "That really did him in. He believed in the importance of factory farming with every kernel of his being."

Green Giant is survived by his son, Little Sprout, the product of a mixed vegetable marriage to a white asparagus.

HE WAS A LUMBERJACK, AND HE'S NOT OK

ST. PAUL, Minn. (*St. Paul Pioneer Press*) — Lumberjack extraordinaire Paul Bunyan died yesterday several months after suffering a massive coronary.

Bunyan had a heart attack early last spring. It took him so long to fall over that everyone in his path had time to get out of the way and move closer to Lambeau Field.

Doctors decided Bunyan needed angioplasty. But Bunyan's arteries were so large, they had to use the tunnel-drilling equipment used from the Ted Williams Tunnel at Boston's Big Dig. Bunyan's condition got dramatically worse because of the tunnel crew showing up ten years late.

Treating Bunyan was a difficult task. In order to allow Bunyan to relieve himself, the hospital staff used a bedpan that was made from the hull of a coal ship.

Every day for breakfast, Bunyan wanted a stack of flapjacks as tall as a man. The hospital didn't have a kitchen big enough to make the order. So, every morning, orderlies had to pour flapjack batter into a large cask and cook it in the CAT scan.

Taking Bunyan's temperature required 20 nurses and a tanker truck of Vaseline. One time, just as they inserted the thermometer, Bunyan sneezed. It was launched all of the way to Toronto, where it is now known as the CN Tower.

In spite of their best efforts, doctors were unable to save Bunyan. He was too big to bury, so they covered him with dirt and opened Giant's Ridge ski resort. Every year, a handful of skiers are lost when they fall into his nostrils.

Killer Sandwich Recipe from Blondie Bumstead's Kitchen

Caterer Served Cold Cut Buffet at Husband's Wake; You Can Too!

ARCATA, Calif. (AP) — Professional caterer and recent widow Blondie Bumstead serves up this tantalizing recipe for the sandwich that her husband ate at least twice a week.

Combine:

Two slices rye bread
1 pound sliced ham
1 pound sliced turkey
1 pound sliced rare roast beef
1 pound sliced salami
1 pound sliced mortadella
1 pound Swiss cheese
1 cup mayonnaise
3 tablespoons peanut butter
6 anchovies
4 pickled herring
4 lettuce leaves
3 tablespoons pickle relish
3 tablespoons deviled ham spread
5 thick-sliced onions
8 pieces hickory-smoked bacon
2 tablespoons hot mustard
1 can black olives
1 bottle hot peppers, drained
salt and pepper
pickle and olive garnish

MAKES 1 SERVING

INTESTINAL BLOCKAGE CLAIMS LIFE OF DAGWOOD BUMSTEAD, 51

ARCATA, Calif. (AP) — Autopsy results show that Dithers Construction employee Dagwood Bumstead died of severe intestinal blockage, according to Rex Morgan, M.D.

He leaves behind wife Blondie, son Alexander, daughter Cookie, and 14 pounds of cold cuts. Bumstead will be buried in his favorite position: lying on his side in a coffin shaped like a couch.

Epicurean-Wannabe Tuna Found Floating in Own Juices

StarKist Spokesman: "Sorry, Charlie"

FT. LAUDERDALE, Fla. (AP) — Charlie the Tuna is dead. A cod by birth, the longtime spokesfish for StarKist was a veteran of more than 80 television commercials. But he was often at odds with his employer. Charlie was on a lifelong mission to develop good taste, while management merely wanted a tuna that tasted good. His career floundered for decades.

The bespectacled icon succumbed to a case of mercury poisoning brought on by a habit of bottom-feeding. The StarKist Company is casting a wide net for friends of the departed who wish to participate in a memorial service. Canning will be private.

Spuds MacKenzie Killed by Drunk Driver

ST. LOUIS, Mo. — Famous bull terrier Spuds MacKenzie was struck down last night during his evening walk. The driver was un-named, but police identified him as a 16-year-old boy who had con-sumed a case of Lite Beer. The teen was only .001 over the legal blood alcohol limit but very, very bloated.

Dog-sized Hawaiian shirt and sunglasses
Worn by Spuds MacKenzie in TV ad — Some pee stains but otherwise clean

Current Bid:	**$.99**
Time left:	7h 12m 33s
Shipping:	US $6.00 Standard Flat Rate Shipping Service
Ships to:	Worldwide
Item location:	San Jose, CA, United States
Quantity:	1

OTHER ITEMS AVAILABLE:

Wardrobe:	Bikini tops and slacks from ad shoot Worn by models partying with Spuds *Some pee stains on pant legs, but otherwise clean*
Props:	Beer cooler, pool umbrella, blanket *Light pee stains but like new*

BUY IT NOW

12:23am, July 5
NAPLES FLORIDA CHIEF OF POLICE
APB

The Naples, Florida, Police Dept. has issued an
All Points Bulletin to be on the lookout for a van
filled with hippies. The vehicle is distinguished by
psychedelic blue and green waves of color, orange
daisies, and "Mystery Machine" painted on the side.
Last seen at Naples Fishing Pier in possession of
hallucinogenic snacks, possibly containing hashish or
peyote.

Local developer Montague Shifty filed complaints
about kids meddling in his plans to demolish an
historic Art Deco building. Has offered reward for
information.

Ringleader appears to be white male, approximate age
25, lanky, with long brown hippy hair and beatnik-
style goatee.

Accomplices, also in their twenties, include tall
blonde effete male, bookish woman in sensible shoes,
and skinny redhead with red lipstick. May be carrying
snacks in common Ziploc bags.

Naples Veterinary Crimes Unit has recovered the body
of overdose victim, a Great Dane with red collar.
Investigating possibility that dead dog is famed
cartoon celebrity Marmaduke.

WILL HUNTING, 66

Local Janitor's Death Reveals Long-Sought Math Proofs

BY CAROL MARTINEZ

When Sara Hunting open her deceased husband's safe deposit box, she found many of the things most widows find. A little cash, the life insurance policy, and his will. But Sara found something more. A collection of papers containing very complicated math formulas.

Her husband, Will, had died just a few weeks ago. They had been together for over 45 years. She knew he liked to stay up nights solving what he called "puzzles" at the kitchen table.

At first, she took the papers from the deposit box to the local high school math teacher. He said they looked like her husband enjoyed drawing mathematical symbols but that they didn't mean anything. Unsatisfied, she took the papers to Professor Sean Fields at Youngstown Community College. Mr. Fields recognized the writings as some sort of mathematical proofs and sent a copy to colleagues of his at MIT. There,

Professor Gerald Lambeau declared that these are not just mathematical proofs but are proofs of five of the most challenging unproven theories in all of mathematics: the Hodge Conjecture, Navier-Stokes Equations, the Reimann Hypothesis, Yang-Mills Theory, and the P vs. NP Problem. The mathematical community couldn't find words to express how it felt.

In 1998, Mr. Hunting set out from Boston in an old Chevy Nova, bound for California. At the end of a long first day, he stopped at a diner for a meal, where his future wife waited on him. "I was wearing my blue uniform—the one with the low-cut front. He noticed me, and I couldn't take my eyes off him," said Mrs. Hunting. "When I was clearing his table, I spilled soup in his lap. I instinctively started to wipe it off. That's when our eyes met. He came home with me that night."

continued on page 7

continued from page 4

Mr. Hunting decided to stay with Sara for a few days before resuming his trip. A few days turned into a few weeks, and Hunting washed dishes at the diner to make a little money. Six weeks later, Sara discovered she was pregnant. They married two months later and Mr. Hunting took a job as janitor at Youngstown Community College, were he worked for his remaining 45 years.

It took a while for others to understand it, but Mr. Hunting knew what he had in those papers. In his will, he bequeathed the mathematical treasure to the Youngstown Community College Math Department.

TAYLOR, OLDEST LIVING HUMAN IN CAPTIVITY, DEAD AT 53

APE CITY (*Simian Gazette*) — Taylor, the human who researchers once believed had a vocabulary of over 500 words, is dead. He had made headlines in the early 2540s when he appeared to testify at his own trial. The hoax was achieved by clever handlers who trained him to ape a handful of legal terms in response to rehearsed questions.

Taylor had been brought into captivity during a standard human round up outside of Ape City. His attentive stare caught the attention of Dr. Zira, a veterinarian who specialized in the study of humans. She attempted to show that Taylor was a vastly superior type of human with special abilities, without success.

Taylor was given to the National Space Administration, which was seeking a human guinea pig for test flights. Taylor's first test nearly ended in disaster. Once in the craft, he started randomly turning dials and flipping switches, nearly launching the ship. The NSA decided that humans lacked the aptitude for space flight and chose to use dogs instead.

Taylor then spent many years in a consumer product–testing laboratory. He was the subject of testing that spared simians from a new eye drop that proved to be excruciatingly painful. He was also the subject of tests that rejected a combined shampoo and conditioner, which resulted in hair loss.

At times, Taylor would embarrass his handlers by repeating phrases he overheard during their reproductive sessions, such as "Take your stinking paws off me, you damn dirty ape."

Rumors persisted that Taylor was able to speak, which resulted in the trial. Afterward, Taylor was placed in the care of famous speech pathologist Dr. Koko.

Dr. Koko, a gorilla, spent years studying the human's cognitive and verbal abilities. In his final assessment, he concluded that while Taylor exhibited a highly developed talent to mimic ape conversation, he did not understand the meaning behind what he was saying.

Taylor spent the last 20 years of his life on display at the Bronx Zoo, where he enjoyed watching television and throwing his feces at visitors.

DR. LEONARD McCOY, 82

Scotty Finally Gets to Say: "He's Dead, Jim."

EARTH (*The Federation Crier*, Star Date 2308.9) — Lieutenant Commander Leonard McCoy, who often referred to himself as "An old country doctor, not a miracle worker!" is presumed dead by the crew of the Starship Enterprise. When engineer Montgomery Scott beamed Dr. McCoy back to the ship from a party on Talos IV, the only matter on the transporter platform was a pile of bones.

Initial findings by Federation investigators point to three possible culprits: the presence of a weak deflector shield, a defective carrier wave, or a stray piece of aluminum foil from Scotty's takeout order of haggis.

Captain James T. Kirk had a dramatic response to the death of his friend: "I...don't know...what...to...say, Scotty. Must...get a grip...on myself..."

The beautiful Lt. Uhura batted her eyelashes and, after communicating the event to Starfleet Command, played a lament on the Vulcan Lyre.

Lt. Sulu was thoughtful in his response:

In a bright meadow
You saved me with a needle
That went whoosh. Goodbye.

Enterprise colleague Mr. Spock, speaking from a resort on Romulus, reacted to the loss of his friend in an uncharacteristically emotional manner: "Fascinating. Humans die."

Interrogation Report
Subject: Uncle Martin
Location: Camp Delta, Guantanamo Bay

TOP SECRET

We have terminated the interrogation of the alien identified as "Uncle Martin." No information was obtained regarding Martian plans to attack or invade Earth.

Because of the critical security nature of this matter, enhanced interrogation techniques were approved by the attorney general for use on the detainee.

The subject was turned in for questioning by one Tim O'Hara of Los Angeles, Calif. Mr. O'Hara reported that the alien had eavesdropped on his thoughts, ruined a relationship with his girlfriend, and was no longer his favorite Martian.

One valuable piece of information was acquired during the interrogation: the gag response of Martians is much more violent than that of humans. Accordingly, waterboarding may be of limited utility against this species.

The body will be sent to Area 51 for a standard alien autopsy.

MAN FALLS OFF TREADMILL WHILE WALKING DOG

Falls Eight Miles to His Death on Planet Below

George Jetson, Dead at 42

HAROLD, 35

MINOR DETAIL LEADS TO ARTIST'S DEMISE

PORTLAND, Ore. (AP) — The artist, who simply called himself "Harold," was killed this week in a bizarre accident while creating an installation at the new "Zooseum" adjacent to the 3D Center of Art and Photography. Known for virtually inventing the bald and black turtleneck look so popular with poseurs, Harold has installations at the Getty, MoMA, the Guggenheim in Bilbao, and Prince's house in Minneapolis.

Harold had just completed drawing a virtual zoo in his signature purple hue, as commissioned by the city of Portland. Using his famous *Crayon Pourpre* technique and working alone in his taciturn manner, Harold filled the stark white walls of the vast space with beautiful and exotic animals. There were monkey cages, reptile terrariums, and an aviary.

Harold was putting the finishing touches on the piece when tragedy struck. He forgot to draw a lock on the lion's cage.

RUDOLPH, FAMED REINDEER, 65

NORTH POLE (AP) — Rudolph the Red-Nosed Reindeer died this week in the Claus retirement stables after an extended illness. Rudolph rocketed to worldwide notoriety when Santa selected him to join his regular team of reindeer for their Christmas Eve journey.

Contrary to the popular stories, Rudolph did not have a red nose. In fact, the red glow emanated from a small patch on the top of his muzzle. Rudolph was one of many reindeer produced by the Mutigent Genetics Corporation (NASDAQ: MGCORP) that had been engaged by Santa to develop genetically enhanced reindeer.

Greg Mendel, chief engineer for MGC recalled, "We weren't trying to make them glow, we were trying to give them scales like fish. The biggest problem you have with flying reindeer is the fur. It ruins the airflow. Scales are aerodynamically superior.

"We had some success and were able to create small patches here and there on a number of reindeer. The surprise was that some of these patches exhibited bioluminescent qualities. Then, we realized we had been using DNA from myctophids, which most people know as 'lantern fish.'"

MGC had produced several of the luminescent reindeer, or "Lumies," as they were called. In the famous story of Rudolph's life, it is suggested that other reindeer bullied him because of his red nose. But 126-year-old stablehand Elf Flow remembers it differently: "Actually, the GM reindeer are about 40 pounds heavier than the regular ones, all muscle, and have no trouble kicking their butts at the reindeer games. Of course, additional weight is not what you want in flying reindeer, and the Lumies were never considered for Christmas flights."

That is, not until that famous foggy Christmas Eve. Concerned about the fog conditions and noticing one of his Lumies standing by, Santa thought it would be a good idea to ask one of them to guide the sleigh. Noticing that Rudolph's luminescent patch was on his nose, Santa picked him. In the popular version of the story, Rudolph saves the day. In fact, the trip did not go so smoothly.

Crew Chief Elf Eddie recalls: "Oh, Santa was pissed. He thought a red light would help guide the way. Problem is red doesn't cut through fog—just reflects off everything.

Santa flew around the world that night surrounded by a red haze and couldn't see a damn thing." Mendel agreed: "The very next day Claus was over in our labs asking for modifications. We worked like crazy for something in the yellow-white spectrum and we're making good progress." But by that time, the legend had been born and Rudolph had gone down in history.

Rudolph died of Dermocystidium, a rare but severe fish skin disease. He was 65.

Grandmother, 74

Was Walking Home from Grandchildren's House on Christmas Eve

By Mel Elmo

Suffern, NY (AP) — A local grandmother was killed in a tragic holiday-related accident last evening. Tracks in the snow near the body were identified as those of reindeer. Police say Grandma had been drinking eggnog before she went out into the snowy night.

Grandma's husband has been taking it well, according to the family, keeping himself busy watching football, playing cards, and drinking beer.

OWNER OF BUILDING & LOAN MISSING AND PRESUMED DEAD

BANKER ADMITS TO AVENGING FORECLOSURE VICTIMS

CLAIMS THEY HAVEN'T HAD SUCH A WONDERFUL LIFE AFTER BEING SWINDLED BY SUBPRIME LOAN OFFICER

BEDFORD FALLS, N.Y. (UPI) — George Bailey, 89, of 320 Sycamore Road, Bedford Falls, is missing and presumed dead.

Anthony Martini, 31, is being held on kidnapping and manslaughter charges. Martini turned himself into authorities yesterday after admitting that he pushed Bailey off a bridge in anger. The young man confronted the head of Bailey Building & Loan after his grandfather received foreclosure notices on his home and bar.

Clarence Oddbody reported to Bert the Cop that he witnessed the skirmish and saw Bailey go over the railing. Oddbody dived in to the river and attempted to save Bailey, to no avail.

Bailey had written scores of subprime loans for his customers on the advice of his nephew, New York investment banker Harry Bailey Jr. The Lehman Brothers banker is a key figure in the collapse of mortgage-backed securities. He is rumored to have convinced members of the Federal Reserve to lower the federal funds rate to 1 percent, which caused home prices to soar, creat-

George Bailey (right) with unidentified man

ing the so-called housing bubble. Harry single-handedly invented "credit default swaps" and made millions stuffing portfolios with collateralized debt obligations. In other words, Harry Bailey Jr., is a scoundrel.

George Bailey's children say their father knew nothing of the massive conspiracy to swindle American investors. The little profits he made from the Building & Loan business were invested for his retirement with a reputable Manhattan firm, Bear Stearns.

184

BELOVED PHILANTHROPIST AND HUMANITARIAN EBENEZER SCROOGE, 92

Had Barely a Penny Left for Himself

BY JOHN HUFFAM

Ebenezer Scrooge passed away peacefully at his nephew's home this week after years of utter selflessness. Once considered a penny pincher, Scrooge suffered a baffling reversal nearly 30 years ago, becoming a savior of sick children, curer of diseases, abolisher of workhouses, and bon vivant partygoer.

Since Boxing Day in 1863, Mr. Scrooge dispersed an estimated one million pounds sterling to charities, poor individuals, and families.

By 1867, Scrooge had sold his flat and started sleeping at his office, sporting bedclothes and slippers during business hours. Londoners concluded that Scrooge had become quite mad. Business partner Robert Cratchit sought to dissolve their partnership in order to halt the old man's zealous distribution of the company's profits to the needy. Scrooge reportedly swore to Cratchit he'd "haunt him from the grave" if he interfered with his philanthropic pursuits.

According to disgruntled junior partner Tim Cratchit, Scrooge's largesse had put the Cratchit family on wobbly financial footing. Shortly before his death, Mr. Scrooge was examined by Dr. Noel Fezziwig of St. Nicholas Hospital for the Mildly Disturbed. The physician pronounced him "Blissfully sound in mind and spirit," a diagnosis which led Mr. Cratchit to request a second opinion. "Well, he is a bit smelly too," the doctor replied.

In his will, Scrooge requested that his epitaph read: "Here Lies Ebenezer Scrooge. May His Name Summon the Spirit of Generosity."

DOUGLAS "DOOGIE" HOWSER, MD, 36

LOS ANGELES (AP) — Douglas "Doogie" Howser died of exhaustion at the Los Angeles hospital where he had been working for more than 20 years straight, with no vacations.

Howser graduated from Princeton University at 10 and finished Harvard Medical School before he turned 15. His parents, both professors of comparative literature at UCLA, considered Doogie an underachiever because he still lived at home.

Friends say the boyishly handsome boy held crushes on various nurses, which could never be reciprocated because of state law. Doogie's hobbies included learning, scoring unusually high on tests, attending yearly MENSA conventions, and working 36-hour shifts in the emergency room.

Doogie's brain was donated to the UCLA medical center for scientific study. It is hoped that a cure could be found for his PSD, known in the medical world as Prodigal Son Disorder. The disease is not passed on genetically because PSD sufferers usually die virgins.

The chief administrator of L.A. General Hospital asked that in lieu of flowers, ambitious and competitive parents continue to push their children into the hospital's residency program. "There's one bunk that just opened," said the official.

ARTHUR HERBERT FONZARELLI, 62

Bowling Accident Claims Life of Beloved Greaser

MILWAUKEE, Wis. (*Milwaukee Sentinel*) — Arthur "Fonzie" Fonzarelli, captain of the "Aaay" team at Cunningham Lanes, died Saturday while competing at the Ralph Malph Punch-in-the-Mouth Classic.

Fonzarelli had a storied career as a mechanic. After demonstrating that he could repair any object by merely applying a precise blow, he quit his job and moved on to more lucrative work. The Fonz specialized in television and appliance repair. Following an appearance on *Fernwood Tonight*, Mr. Fonzarelli was in great demand to repair all manner of sophisticated technical equipment, primarily supercomputers, air-traffic-control radars, and MRI machines. The highlight of his career was in 2006, when the Fonz flew aboard NASA's Shuttle Endeavor to repair the Hubble telescope. NASA engineers designed a special glove which would allow him to both

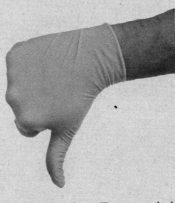

effectively strike the device and give the thumbs-up sign.

But not all of Fonzie's repairs ended successfully. He once broke his hand fixing an Abrams M1 tank that the Army couldn't start (it started). He accidentally added one second to the year 2000 by hitting the Atomic Clock too hard. And Mr. Fonzarelli had just made a "minor adjustment" to the control panel of the Three Mile Island nuclear power plant before its partial meltdown in 1979.

Bowling tournament–goers say the Fonz needed to pick up a split in the seventh frame when his favorite ball got stuck in the pneumatic bowling ball return apparatus. Angered, he stared into the hole and hit the side of the machine in frustration. The ball shot out, striking Fonzie in the face. Dr. Potsie Weber pronounced him dead at the scene.

Fonzarelli will be buried with his motorcycle and comb.

About the Authors

BARRY NELSON was born in the Jersey Shore city of Long Branch, the birthplace of Bruce Springsteen, Dorothy Parker, and Robert Pinsky. Finally, somebody from that town has amounted to something. He attended Seton Hall University long enough to meet Tom and stumble down the wrong career path. A philosophy degree might have been more lucrative.

Barry was a radio producer and host before becoming a fundraiser for public radio and television. While developing a pilot for a public radio food show, he interviewed dozens of authors, including Julia Child, for whom he prepared lunch on her trusty Garland stove.

The first page his parents used to turn to each morning was the obituaries. But he wondered why fictional characters didn't get the same treatment as real people, and the idea for this book was born.

Barry lives in Massachusetts with his wife Amy and son Simon, with occasional visits by college-age son Colin. He is director of radio and television on-air fundraising at WGBH in Boston.

TOM SCHECKER grew up in Cincinnati, Ohio. He stayed out of trouble until kindergarten, when he was ordered to stop teaching the other kids Beatles songs–a radical act at the time. He received a debate scholarship to Seton Hall University, where he majored in Incompletes. As a part-time job, he coached a local high school debate team to the state championship.

Tom started temping as a night shift word processor at Goldman Sachs. This led to full-time consulting in the technology department, which lasted fifteen years. He spent the next ten years as an internet consultant to Wall Street firms and start-ups. He is currently the information architect at a global law firm.

Tom lives in the Chelsea section of Manhattan with his partner Karen and a large black dog named Cupcake. He performs standup comedy.